Kada prođe zima,
i dođe lijepi maj.
Djevojke su ljepše
ljubav im daj.
Šetalište tamno
uzdasima zri,
neke oči plove,
neke riječi nježne.

Sad je dječak star
a zima pokri brijeg.
Park i kosa sijedi,
al' otići će snijeg.
Proljeće i mladost
ispuniće dan.
Sarajevo moje,
jedini moj grad.

REF: Bilo gdje....

Prepisivala:
Zlata
Filipović

Kemal Monteno

Zlata's Diary

Zlata Filipović

Zlata's Diary

A CHILD'S LIFE IN SARAJEVO

With an introduction by
Janine Di Giovanni

Translated with notes by
Christina Pribichevich-Zorić

VIKING

VIKING
Published by the Penguin Group
Penguin Books USA Inc., 375 Hudson Street,
New York, New York 10014, U.S.A.
Penguin Books Ltd, 27 Wrights Lane, London W8 5TZ, England
Penguin Books Australia Ltd, Ringwood, Victoria, Australia
Penguin Books Canada Ltd, 10 Alcorn Avenue,
Toronto, Ontario, Canada M4V 3B2
Penguin Books (N.Z.) Ltd, 182–190 Wairau Road,
Auckland 10, New Zealand

Penguin Books Ltd, Registered Offices:
Harmondsworth, Middlesex, England

First American edition
Published in 1994 by Viking Penguin,
a division of Penguin Books USA Inc.

1   3   5   7   9   10   8   6   4   2

Originally published in France as *Le Journal de Zlata* by Fixot et editions
Robert Laffont. Copyright © Fixot et editions Robert Laffont, 1993.
This translation first published in Great Britain by Penguin Books Ltd.

CIP data available
ISBN 0-670-85724-6

Printed in the United States of America
Typeset by Creative Graphics, Allentown, PA
Set in New Baskerville

Introduction

I first heard of Zlata Filipović in the summer of 1993 when a Bosnian friend told me about a young girl who was being called "the Anne Frank of Sarajevo." I found out that Zlata was a thirteen-year-old girl, living with her parents, who had been keeping a diary since September 1991, a few months before the first barricades went up in the city and the heavy shelling began. Before the war broke out, she led a very happy, normal life; she had no way of knowing that within six months her life would change irrevocably. When she began writing her diary, which she called Mimmy, she had no idea that the family weekend house outside Sarajevo would be destroyed; that her best friends would be killed while playing in a park. She only thought about things that any normal thirteen-year-old girl thinks about: pop music, movies, boys, Linda Evangelista and Claudia Schiffer, skiing in the mountains outside Sarajevo and her next holiday in Italy or at the beach. Her family was comfortably well-off, the apartment in which her parents had lived for twenty years was spacious and elegant with a view of the river, and they had neighbors, relatives and friends nearby who were constantly dropping in.

Life changed quickly in the spring of 1992. Within a couple of months of Zlata's first diary entry, Serbian artillery positions were set up on the hills directly above her house and the family had to move all their possessions into the front room, which was protected from shrapnel by sandbags. Soon, there were no more windows left in Zlata's apartment: they were all blown out by the impact of shells. At that point, Bosnians who could leave the city fled; others refused to go, not really believing that their city would be reduced to rubble. Zlata watched with disbelief as her friends and relatives tried desperately to flee before it was too late. "I'm all alone here," she wrote.

Over the next few months, Zlata watched her world fall apart. She could not comprehend the issues that had become all-important: ethnic cleansing, the Geneva talks, Lord Owen and the division of Bosnia. She could only comprehend that nothing was the same and nothing would ever be the same again. Her father, a lawyer whose office was next door to their apartment, stopped working, but eerily, the sign remained on the door which was littered with shrapnel. Her mother, a chemist, began to slip into a state of gloom and despair as the family spent day after day cowering in the cellar while heavy artillery ravaged Sarajevo. Supplies ran low and then became nonexistent. The electricity was cut, the phone went dead, water stopped running from the taps. Food consisted of humanitarian aid packages: tasteless white feta cheese, the occasional loaf of bread if you waited long enough in line and were brave enough to face the shelling, the occasional can of meat bought on the black market for 50 Deutsche Marks. There was no water to take a bath or flush a toilet. The only way to get it was to stand in a water line under frequent shell-fire. Her parents lost so much weight that they could not wear any of their old clothes. Zlata told me that "I gained some because I am still growing." She could not remember when she'd last eaten an egg, a piece of fruit.

Before the war, she had been a diligent student studying English, music, math and literature, but because the Serbs often targeted schools and playgrounds, school was stopped—it was too dangerous to walk the few blocks to attend classes. Zlata was not allowed to go outside and play, so she had to stay in the apartment. Whenever it seemed safe, she would practice the piano, which was in her parents' bedroom—one of the more dangerous rooms. She played Bach and Chopin even while the sound of machine guns echoed from the hills. It gave her comfort to know that, despite the war, her playing was improving. For a short while, it also made her forget that outside in the streets below her, a war was being fought. And all the time, she kept on writing about her daily life.

During the summer of 1993, Zlata submitted her diaries to a teacher, who had them published by a small press in Sarajevo with the help of UNICEF. She became an instant celebrity, with packs of journalists and television crews climbing the stairs to her apartment to quiz the small girl about her life. Zlata responded graciously in her careful schoolgirl English. She had lost so many of her friends that she became friendly with some of the journalists. But journalists do not stay for long in Sarajevo, and whenever one left Zlata suffered a feeling of loss.

I first met Zlata when her school temporarily restarted last autumn. A small figure with bright blue eyes bounded up to me enthusiastically with an outstretched hand and addressed me in English. We sat on a wall and when a shell fell I noticed that she did not flinch. As we walked to her house, she talked about her life, her dreams, her sadness. She told me about the death of Nina, a friend she had known since she was very young and who had been killed. "How many of your friends have died?" I asked her gently. She thought for a moment. "Too many to count," she replied. I thought then that she seemed more adult, more resigned and stoical, than most of the adults I knew.

In October, during one of the worst days of shelling, I drove to Zlata's house to make sure that the family was all right. Her mother answered the door; she was shaking with fear. "We were in the basement all morning," she said, and her voice broke. She sat on the sofa in the "safe room" and collapsed into sobs. Zlata and I stood by watching helplessly while she wept for half an hour. "No more, no more, we cannot bear any more." I gave her a cigarette, but her hand shook so heavily that she could not bring it to her lips; her foot tapped violently against the bare floor. I sat on the floor with Zlata beside me, but there was little I could say. Certainly not "I understand," because I did not—as a journalist, I was able to leave Sarajevo at free will—and certainly not "Don't worry, the war will end soon," because we would have known that it was a lie.

At one point, I turned around to see Zlata. I placed my hand on her shoulder and asked, "Are you all right?" She looked at me gravely and said, "I have to be all right." Her voice was very old and it chilled me. Not only had she lost her innocence, those wonderful years when she should have been meeting boys and laughing with her girlfriends, but she was in the terrible reversed position of having to be strong for the sake of her parents. Even if she wanted to, she could not fall apart.

That afternoon, Zlata's mother asked me if I would drive to a very dangerous part of town to make sure her sister was still alive. Her family lived in an area where the shelling was intense. I said I would, because I had access that day to an armored car. But the area was deep in the territory of a warlord who was notorious for stealing cars and flak jackets and for dragging Bosnians out of their cars and forcing them to dig trenches. My driver, who had Serb identification, refused to go and told me it was suicide if I did. Frustrated, I abandoned the attempt and drove back. I used my Deutsche Marks to buy all I could find on the black market: the selection was pathetic, but I knew that Zlata and her parents would welcome anything. So I climbed the stairs to their apartment with a few bags of wilted vegetables, a few cans of Coke, some chocolate, a few cans of meat, some candles. When I entered the room, the family's eyes lit up: as though, instead of a few onions, I had brought a turkey from

Harrods. When I talked to Zlata later about food, she reminisced about all the wonderful things that she used to eat, and then laughing, said, "Stop! That's enough!" The memory of walking through the streets of the old town of Sarajevo and stopping for a pizza or spaghetti ("real spaghetti, with meat and cheese, not the kind of spaghetti we have now, with nothing on it") was too painful to bear for a thirteen year-old who existed on rice and beans.

We sat on her bed in her bedroom decorated with posters of supermodels, and she showed me family pictures of a different world: Zlata as a baby being held by her grandmother, Zlata and her mother outside the beloved weekend house, Zlata and her father on the beach in Italy. There was one faded picture of two small children standing in a park. She stared at it and said, "That's my friend Nina. We were playing in the same park that she was killed in." Before turning the page, she paused over the photograph, touching it as though she could touch her friend.

Zlata is an only child, treasured and protected by her parents. Perhaps it was the confidence inspired by her family life that gave her the will to endure the horrors that were taking place on her doorstep. During the course of reporting the war in Bosnia, I met many children, sat with them in the hospital, in their homes, in orphanages. All of them were traumatized and shell-shocked. I spoke to psychiatrists who talked of post-traumatic stress syndrome and the effect of the war on all these children. Zlata was different: she was suffering, but because she was recording the events taking place around her, she tended to see the world from a slightly detached viewpoint. It was almost as though she was watching a film in which she was a character. There are hundreds of thousands like her in Bosnia: besieged, frightened, their short lives suddenly ground to a halt. The difference is that Zlata kept a careful record of the chilling events—the deaths, the mutilations, the sufferings. When we read her diaries, we think of desperation, of confusion and of innocence lost, because a child should not be seeing, should not be living with this kind of horror. Her tragedy becomes our tragedy because we know what is happening in Sarajevo. And still, we do not act.

I wrote about Zlata in the *Sunday Times* [London] and shortly afterward, I received this letter from an eight-year-old in Glasgow, which she asked me to forward to Zlata:

Dear Zlata,
I feel sorry about your friend Nina. I wish the war would stop. I don't see the point of having wars.

When my mum read me the interview you gave Janine di Giovanni, I was really interested. I thought you sounded like a nice person. I would like to be your pen-pal. I live in Glasgow, in Scotland. Hope you have a merry Christmas and no shooting or shelling in the new year.

Yours sincerely,

Helen Harvey

Unfortunately, there was increased shelling and shooting on Christmas Day and over the New Year in Sarajevo. Five children were killed when a kindergarten was shelled by the Serbs.

However, on December 23, 1993, Zlata and her parents were transported from their home in the Skenderija district of old Sarajevo in two armored vehicles of the French UNPROFOR contingent and taken through government and Serb checkpoints at the airport. A few hours later, they left for the safety of Paris on a UN plane.

As I watched the television images of Sarajevo at Christmas, I remember Zlata telling me about her dreams and I wonder what she is dreaming now, safe in Paris. "I used to dream about the beach, somewhere warm," she once told me. "But when there is shelling, I only think about being safe." She is now safe, but there are thousands of other children who are not, who are sitting in the dark around a candle, hungry, terrified by the shelling, who have lost parents, brothers, sisters. It is for them that Zlata wrote this book.

JANINE DI GIOVANNI
London 1994

Zlata Filipović's Family and Friends

ZLATA'S FAMILY

Malik
HER FATHER

Alica
HER MOTHER

Melica
HER FATHER'S SISTER

Braco and Seka
BRACO IS HER MOTHER'S BROTHER; HE IS
MARRIED TO SEKA AND THEY ARE THE PARENTS
OF MIKICA AND DAČO

FRIENDS OF ZLATA
AND HER PARENTS

Kemo and Alma
NEIGHBORS; PARENTS OF HARIS AND NEJRA.
RELATIVES OF NEIGHBORS EMINA AND SAMRA

Bobar Family
CLOSE NEIGHBORS AND FAMILY FRIENDS.
GRANDMA MIRA, AUNTIE BODA AND UNCLE
ŽIKA; MAJA AND BOJANA, THEIR DAUGHTERS

Emina and Samra
NEIGHBORS AND FRIENDS; RELATIVES OF
KEMO AND ALMA

Irena
SUMMER SCHOOL TEACHER

Ivanka
MOTHER'S FRIEND FROM WORK

Braco and Keka Lajtner
HUSBAND AND WIFE; PARENTS OF MARTINA
AND MATEA

Mirna
ZLATA'S BEST FRIEND

Mišo
MIRNA'S FATHER

Mladjo
SRDJAN'S BROTHER

Neda
MOTHER'S BEST FRIEND FROM WORK

Nedo
TWENTY-SEVEN-YEAR-OLD REFUGEE, FRIEND
AND NEIGHBOR

Radmila
MOTHER'S FRIEND FROM WORK

Slobo and Doda
HUSBAND AND WIFE; FRIENDS OF ZLATA'S
MOTHER; PARENTS OF DEJAN

Srdjan and Bokica
HUSBAND AND WIFE; FRIENDS OF ZLATA'S
PARENTS; PARENTS OF ANDREJ AND VANJA

Zlata's Diary

Monday, September 2, 1991

Behind me—a long, hot summer and the happy days of summer holidays; ahead of me—a new school year. I'm starting fifth grade. I'm looking forward to seeing my friends at school, to being together again. Some of them I haven't seen since the day the school bell rang, marking the end of term. I'm glad we'll be together again, and share all the worries and joys of going to school.

Mirna, Bojana, Marijana, Ivana, Maša, Azra, Minela, Nadža—we're all together again.

Tuesday, September 10, 1991

The week was spent getting my books and school supplies, describing how we spent our holidays on the seaside, in the mountains, in the countryside and abroad. We all went somewhere and we all have so much tell one another.

Thursday, September 19, 1991

Classes have also started at music school now. I go twice a week for piano and solfeggio. I'm continuing my tennis lessons. Oh yes, I've been moved up to the "older" group in tennis. Wednesdays I go to Auntie Mika's for English lessons. Tuesdays I have choir practice. Those are my responsibilities. I have six lessons every day, except Fridays. I'll survive . . .

Monday, September 23, 1991

I don't know if I mentioned my workshop class (it's a new subject) which starts in fifth grade. Our teacher is Jasmina Turajlić and I LIKE HER. We learn about wood, what it is, how it's used, and it's pretty interesting. Soon we'll be moving on to practical work, which means making various things out of wood and other materials. It'll be interesting.

The teachers have already started testing us, there's history, geography, biology. I have to study!

Friday, September 27, 1991

I'm home from school and I'm really tired. It's been a hard week. Tomorrow is Saturday and I can sleep as long as I like. LONG LIVE SATURDAYS! Tomorrow night, I'm "busy." Tomorrow is Ivana Varunek's birthday party. I received an invitation today. More about this next time . . .

Sunday, September 29, 1991

It's now 11:00 A.M. Ivana's birthday is actually today but

she had her party yesterday. It was super. There were little rolls, things to munch on, sandwiches and, most important of all—a cake. Boys were invited as well as girls. We had a dance contest and I won. My prize was a little "jewelry" box. All in all it was a great party.

Sunday, October 6, 1991
I'm watching the American Top 20 on MTV. I don't remember a thing, who's in what place.

I feel great because I've just eaten a "Four Seasons" PIZZA with ham, cheese, ketchup and mushrooms. It was yummy. Daddy bought it for me at Galija's (the pizzeria around the corner). Maybe that's why I didn't remember who took what place—I was too busy enjoying my pizza.

I've finished studying and tomorrow I can go to school BRAVELY, without being afraid of getting a bad grade. I deserve a good grade because I studied all weekend and I didn't even go out to play with my friends in the park. The weather is nice and we usually play "monkey in the middle," talk and go for walks. Basically, we have fun.

Friday, October 11, 1991
A hard but successful working day. Math test—A,

written test in language—A, biology oral—A. I'm tired, but happy.

Another weekend ahead of me. We're going to Crnotina (our place about fifteen kilometers away)—it has a big orchard with a house that's about 150 years old—a cultural monument under protection of the state. Mommy and Daddy restored it. Grandma and Granddad are still there. I miss them. I miss Vildana, her dog Ati, I miss the clean air and beautiful countryside.

Sunday, October 13, 1991

It was wonderful in Crnotina. I like our house (it's really unusual) and the surrounding countryside more and more every time we go. We picked pears, apples, walnuts, we took pictures of a clever little squirrel that stole the walnuts, in the evening we had a barbecue—my specialty is *ćevapčići* [grilled meat rolls]. Grandma made apple strudel. I collected different leaves for the herbarium and played with Ati.

Autumn has already replaced summer. Slowly but surely it is painting and coloring nature with its brush. The leaves are turning yellow, red, and they are falling. The days are getting shorter and it's colder. Autumn is really nice too! In fact, every season's nice in its own way. Somehow I don't notice and don't feel the beauty of nature when I'm in town the way I do when I'm in Crnotina. In Crnotina it smells good, it caresses me, it calls me into its embrace. I had a really nice rest enjoying and feeling the beauty of nature.

Saturday, October 19, 1991

Yesterday was a really awful day. We were ready to go to Jahorina (the most beautiful mountain in the world) for the weekend. But when I got home from school, I found my mother in tears and my father in uniform. I had a lump in my throat when Daddy said he had been called up by the police reserve. I hugged him, crying, and started begging him not to go, to stay at home. He said he had to go. Daddy went, and Mommy and I were left alone. Mommy cried and phoned friends and relatives. Everyone came immediately (Slobo, Doda, Keka, Mommy's brother Braco, Aunt Melica, there were so many I can't remember them all). They all came to console us and to offer their help. Keka took me to spend the night with Martina and Matea. When I woke up in the morning, Keka told me everything was all right and that Daddy would be home in two days.

I'm home now, Melica is staying with us and it

looks as though everything will be all right. Daddy should be home the day after tomorrow. ~~Thank God!~~

Tuesday, October 22, 1991

Everything really does seem to have turned out all right. Daddy got back yesterday, on his birthday. He's off again tomorrow, and then every two days. He'll be on duty for ten hours each time. We'll just have to get used to it. I suppose it won't last for long. But, I don't know what it all means. Some reservists from Montenegro have entered Herzegovina. Why? For what? Politics, it seems, but I don't understand politics. After Slovenia and Croatia, are the winds of war now blowing toward Bosnia-Herzegovina??? No, that's impossible.

Wednesday, October 23, 1991

There's a real war going on in Dubrovnik. It's being badly shelled. People are in shelters, they have no water, no electricity, the phones aren't working. We see horrible pictures on TV. Mommy and Daddy are worried. Is it possible that such a beautiful town is being destroyed? Mommy and Daddy are especially fond of it. It was there, in the Ducal Palace, that they picked up a quill and wrote "YES" to spending the rest of their lives together. Mommy says it's the most beautiful town in the world and it mustn't be destroyed!!!

We're worried about Srdjan (my parents' best friend who lives and works in Dubrovnik, but his family is still in Sarajevo) and his parents. How are they coping with everything that's happening over there? Are they alive? We're trying to talk to him with the help of a ham radio, but it's not working. Bokica (Srdjan's wife) is miserable. Every attempt to get some news ends in failure. Dubrovnik is cut off from the rest of the world.

Wednesday, October 30, 1991

Good news from my piano teacher today. There's going to be a school recital and I'll be playing in it!!! I have to practice. I'll be playing Kabalevsky, *Six Variations on a Slovak Song*. All the variations are short, but difficult. It doesn't matter, I'll do my best.

Nothing new at school, it's the half term soon and we're working on our grades. The days are shorter, it's colder, which means it'll snow soon— HOORAY! Jahorina, skiing, two-seaters, one-seaters, ski-lifts—I can hardly wait!!! I'm pushing it a bit, there's still some time to go, but we've already bought ski tickets for the whole season.

Tuesday, November 5, 1991

I've just come back from choir practice. I'm hoarse! Imagine, our choir teacher told us today that we would be giving a performance soon. What a "public life" I'm having! We'll be singing "Nabucco," "Ave Maria," "When I Went to Bembaša," "I Sing of Thee" and "Ode to Joy." All the songs are wonderful.

Friday, November 8, 1991

I'm packing and I'm putting you, dear Diary, in my backpack. I'm spending the whole weekend with Martina and Matea (M&M). Super!!! Mommy is letting me go. In my backpack I've got my school books, my pajamas, my toothbrush . . . and as soon as I put you in—off I go.
  CIAO!!!

Sunday, November 10, 1991

It's now 4:30 and I've just come home from M&M.

It was wonderful. We played tennis, watched MTV, RTL, SKY . . . went out, walked and had fun. I took you with me, dear Diary, but I didn't write anything. You're not cross with me, are you?

I've done my homework and now I'm going to have a bath, watch TV and then go to bed. A weekend like any other—wonderful!

Tuesday, November 12, 1991

The situation in Dubrovnik is getting worse and worse. We managed to learn through the ham radio that Srdjan is alive and that he and his parents are all right. The pictures on TV are awful. People are starving. We're wondering about how to send a package to Srdjan. It can be done somehow through Caritas.[1] Daddy is still going to the reserves, he comes home tired. When will it stop? Daddy says maybe next week. ~~Thank God.~~

Thursday, November 14, 1991

Daddy isn't going to the reserves anymore. Hooray!!! . . . Now we'll be able to go to Jahorina and Crnotina on weekends. But, gasoline has been

[1] The Catholic humanitarian aid and relief organization.

a problem lately. Daddy often spends hours waiting in the line for gasoline, he goes outside of town to get it, and often comes home without getting the job done.

Together with Bokica we sent a package to Srdjan. We learned through the ham radio that they have nothing to eat. They have no water, Srdjan swapped a bottle of whisky for five liters of water. Eggs, apples, potatoes—the people of Dubrovnik can only dream about them.

War in Croatia, war in Dubrovnik, some reservists in Herzegovina. Mommy and Daddy keep watching the news on TV. They're worried. Mommy often cries looking at the terrible pictures on TV. They talk mostly politics with their friends. What is politics? I haven't got a clue. And I'm not really interested. I just finished watching *Midnight Caller* on TV.

Wednesday, November 20, 1991

I've just come home from music school. I had my school recital. I think I was good. I tried. I made only two mistakes which they might not even have noticed. Matea was in the audience. I'm tired because it was nerve-racking.

It'll be November 29th, Republic Day, soon. Mommy and Daddy are going shopping and are getting everything ready to go to Jaca's (a family friend) and Jahorina.

HOORAY!!! I can hardly wait. Jahorina will be wonderful and unforgettable as always.

We're on Jahorina. Jaca has warmed up the house, there's a fire burning in the fireplace. As usual, Zoka (Jaca's husband) is making something special to eat, Daddy is talking politics with Boža (our friend and Daddy's colleague). Mommy and Jaca keep jumping into the conversation, and we children, Branko, Svjetlana, Nenad, Mirela, Anela, Oga and I, are wondering whether to take a walk, play a game, watch a movie on TV or play the unavoidable Scrabble. This time we've decided to play a game. We always have fun and laugh in our games, we have our own sense of humor. It's cold but wonderful. I'm so happy, I'm having such a good time. The food, drink and company in Jahorina are so nice. And at night, my favorite moment—Oga and I are the first to go to bed—for a long, long talk before going to sleep. We talk, we make plans, we tell each other secrets. Last night we chattered about MTV and the new music video.

Monday, December 2, 1991

It's my birthday tomorrow. Mommy is making a cake and all the rest, because we really celebrate in our house. One day is for my friends, that's December 3, and the next day is for family friends and relatives. Mommy and I are getting a tombola [a basket of party favors] together, and thinking up questions for the children's quiz. This year we have birthday cups, plates and napkins all with little red apples on them. They're sweet. Mommy bought them in Pula. The cake will be shaped like a butterfly and . . . this time I'll be blowing out eleven candles. I'll have to take a deep breath and blow them all out at once.

Tuesday, December 3, 1991

Today is the big day—my birthday. Happy Birthday to Me!!! But, alas, I'm sick. My sinuses are inflamed and some kind of pus is trickling down my throat. Nothing hurts really, but I have to take an antibiotic—Penbritin, and some disgusting nose drops. They sting. Why did this have to happen on my birthday? Oh, I am unlucky! (Don't be such a pessimist, Zlata, things aren't so bad.)

All right, I'll get well and celebrate my birthday later, with my friends, I mean, because the "grown-up" guests (family and family friends) are coming to wish me a happy birthday today. And here I am in my nightgown! Mommy and Daddy gave me a wonderful birthday present—Head skis, new Tyrolia bindings and new poles. Super! Thank you Mommy. Thank you Daddy!!

We've just seen off some of the guests, and I'm tired, I have to stop writing, I've run out of ideas and inspiration. Good night.

Wednesday, December 4, 1991

I'm writing to you from bed, dear Diary. Another day in bed awaits me. Bimbilimbica (my favorite doll) is snoozing on the little table, and Panda just keeps looking and looking at her . . . Let him look.

7:45. I'm in bed again, listening to the rattle of our washing machine. The repairman came to fix it. Poor thing, it's a hundred years old. I should treat it with respect. The repairman has gone and I'm now listening to Michael Jackson, "Man in the Mirror." I just had a crazy idea. I'm going to try to join Madonna's Fan Club. I really am crazy!

Thursday, December 5, 1991

I woke up very late. Then Azra, Minela and Bojana came by to see me. Bojana is having a birthday party on Saturday. Lucky her! WHY AM I SICK??? Boo-hoo! Boo-hoo!

Saturday, December 7, 1991

The weekend in bed. Bojana's having her birthday party today and I can't go. I feel sad. I can't even read or watch TV anymore. I want to get well!

Every night Mommy and Daddy keep trying to get Srdjan on the phone. It's impossible to get through to Dubrovnik. God, there really is a war going on down there. Today I saw pictures of Dubrovnik on TV. Horrible. We're worried about Srdjan and his family. Mommy managed (because she was persistent) to get him on the phone at eleven o'clock last night. He's hungry and thirsty, he's cold, they have no electricity, no water, nothing to eat. He's sad. Mommy cried. What on earth is happening and why? God, is it possible that there's a war going on down there? Dubrovnik is being destroyed, people are dying. Sad but true. Take care of yourself, Srdjan, I'll keep my fingers crossed for you. We'll be sending you another package in a few days, through Caritas.

Zlata, in 1981, one year old. Four years later she is enjoying the Olympic peaks of Jahorina, close to Sarajevo, according to Zlata "the most beautiful mountain in the world."

Zlata celebrates her fifth birthday with friends.
And, at eight, a conscientious music student,
she plays the piano and sings.

On Monday I'm going to Auntie Mira's (the doctor's) for a check-up.

Ciao!!!

Monday, December 9, 1991

I went to see Auntie Mira. She says I can go back to school tomorrow. Whoopee! We bought a pair of gray trousers at "KIKA's" (the children's boutique). I like them. Well, *Murphy Brown* is going to be on TV now. I have to watch!!!

Ciao . . .

Wednesday, December 11, 1991

I'm back at school. There's a lot to learn, it'll be the end of term soon. I've got a math test tomorrow. I have to practice. I got an A in history today. On Saturday I'm celebrating (a bit late) my eleventh birthday.

Saturday, December 14, 1991

Today, eleven days later, I celebrated my eleventh birthday with my girlfriends. It was like the real thing. We had the tombola, the quiz, the "butterfly" cake. I blew out all the candles on my first try. We had a good time. Being sick stopped me from having my party on December 3, but this was nice too. Once again—Happy Birthday to Me, and may I never get sick on this big day again. Oh yes, I got wonderful presents—most of them from "Melanie's" (a boutique with wonderful knick-knacks). They fit in perfectly with everything in my room.

Thursday, December 19, 1991
Sarajevo has launched an appeal (on TV) called "Sarajevo Helps the Children of Dubrovnik." In Srdjan's parcel we put a nice New Year's present for him to give to some child in Dubrovnik. We made up a package of sweets, chocolates, vitamins, a doll, some books, pencils, notebooks—whatever we could manage, hoping to bring happiness to some innocent child who has been stopped by the war from going to school, playing, eating what he wants and enjoying his childhood. It's a nice little package. I hope it makes whoever gets it happy. That's the idea. I also wrote a New Year's card saying I hoped the war in Dubrovnik would end soon.

Thursday, December 26, 1991
5:45. I haven't written to you for a long time, dear

Diary. Okay, let's start from the beginning. I got a B in my piano exam, an A in solfeggio and an A in general music, so I finished with an A average. Super. Mirna did the same as me. I wrote to *Sa-3-Ći-ći* [a children's program] TV show and won a ticket for the Ninja Turtles.

It was Christmas yesterday. We went to M&M's (Martina and Matea's). It was wonderful. A big Christmas tree. Christmas presents and the proverbial Christmas table. And Bokica was there with Andrej. And there was a surprise. Srdjan phoned. Everyone was happy and sad at the same time. There we were all warm, surrounded by Christmas decorations and presents, with lots of wonderful food and drink in front of us. And there he was, like everybody else in Dubrovnik . . . in a war. This war will pass, Srdjan, we'll all be together again! You've got to hold on!!! I'm keeping my fingers crossed for you and for all the people and children in Dubrovnik.

It'll be New Year's Eve soon. The atmosphere seems different than before. Mommy, Daddy and our friends and family aren't planning a New Year's Eve party this year. They don't talk about it much. Is it because of the war in Dubrovnik? Is it some kind of fear? I don't know or understand a thing. Mommy says we'll decorate the tree tomorrow.

Today was my last day at music school this year. And school?! I'm hoping for straight As. YO, BABY, YO!, as The Fresh Prince of Bel Air would say. That's one of my favorite programs on TV. PHEW! I certainly do talk a lot. Just look at all these words. PHEW!

Just one more thing: my class is going to the cinema tomorrow. We're going to see *White Fang*. It's a wonderful book by Jack London, I hope the film is as good.
Ciao!!!

Monday, December 30, 1991

We've decorated the tree. I went shopping with Mommy. We bought presents for the family and friends. We wrapped everything up nicely, wrote everyone a New Year's card and I laid them all out under the tree. Everything looks wonderful. Mommy is cooking, baking—there'll be all sorts of goodies. But I think everybody will be spending New Year's Eve at home.

Wednesday, January 1, 1992

Yes, I spent New Year's Eve AT HOME WITH MY

MOMMY AND DADDY. It wasn't bad, just a bit odd. Happy New Year.

We were alone on New Year's Eve, but today the house is full of people. Lots of visitors, both "small" (my friends) and "big" (Mommy and Daddy's), as well as family. In the end it was fun.

Saturday, January 4, 1992

We went to Jahorina yesterday. It's super there. We rode our sleds in the dark, fooled around, played Yatzee. It was great, really! But we didn't spend the night. Never mind, it doesn't matter. *The Witches of Eastwick* was on yesterday, with Cher, Michelle Pfeiffer, Jack Nicholson and some actress whose name begins with an S. . . . S, s, s, s, s . . . I just can't remember. And another thing. Jaca gave me a polka-dot cap and gloves for my New Year's present. They're so cute. Coochie-coochie-coo!!!

Sunday, January 5, 1992

The cinema was an absolute fiasco. A disaster! Like seeing Jordan from NKOTB [New Kids on the Block]. First of all, we didn't see *White Fang*, we saw *My Brother Aleksa*. We could have survived this if someone hadn't been throwing paper and spitting from the balcony. Of course, I wouldn't be Zlata Filipović if I hadn't been sitting in the first row under that balcony! Naturally! Serves me right for sitting in the wrong place!

Monday, January 13, 1992

We just saw M&M and Neda off. AUHHHH! It's been a long day! I'm off to bed now, it's 11:10. I'm reading *Captain at Fifteen* by Jules Verne.

Everything is the same and keeps going in a circle (in my holiday life). Boredom, books, friends, phone calls and so on. I really do have to go to bed now! GOOD NIGHT AND SWEET DREAMS!

Tuesday, January 14, 1992

I yawned, opened my pen and started to write: I'm listening to the music from *Top Gun* on "Good Vibrations" (on the radio). Something else is on now. I've just destroyed the back page of *Bazaar* [the fashion magazine]. I talked to Mommy on the phone. She's at work.

I have something to tell you. Every night I dream that I'm asking Michael Jackson for his autograph, but either he won't give it to me or his secretary writes it, and then all the letters melt, because Michael Jackson didn't write them. Sad. Poor me. Ha, ha, ha, ha, I have to, ha, ha, ha, ha, laugh, ha, ha, ha, ha.

4:15. I was at Vanja and Andrej's (V&A). There was a bit of trouble at home because I stayed so long. But it took a long time to finish our game of Monopoly. Both Vanja and Andrej went bankrupt, and I had all the red notes (5,000 each). I had 12,000,000, to be exact. Mind you, I had the Place de Genève and Côte d'Azure.

Oops. There's *Bugs Bunny*. I've got to watch!

7:50. I'm watching DIAL MTV:

5. Pet Shop Boys with "Was It Worth It?"

4. I can't remember

3. Nirvana

2. Guns 'n' Roses

1. New Kids on the Block.

Thursday, January 16, 1992

I got up late. Mommy isn't feeling well. She didn't go to work today. Safia (the woman who helps in the house) came. I'm bored. When are we going to go to Jahorina?

Thursday, January 23, 1992

9:55. I'm lying in bed. But not in my bed. THAT'S RIGHT. Dum-di-dum-di-dum. I'm on Jahorina. I've been here seven days now. I'm lying next to Oga. Listening to the buzzing of a boring fly and to the stove, and talking to Oga. We're talking the way we always do in this bed, in this room, on Jahorina.

I haven't written to you for a long time, dear Diary. As soon as I came I was really busy, skiing, nighttime skiing, ice-skating on "Boza's Trail," building snowmen and snow houses. I simply didn't have time. We're all here: Oga, Branko, Svjetlana, Nenad, Bojan, Boris, Mirela, Anela, and, of course, me. You'll forgive me. I know you will. I promise to write more often.

Oga and I are making plans about which ski-lifts to take tomorrow: Ogorjelica I, Ogorjelica II, Šator ... God, such a choice. I can hardly wait.

I AM HAPPY!

Sunday, January 26, 1992

I'm sick. My throat hurts. I have a temperature. I was on fire. It's gone down a bit now, but I have a terrible cough.

Tuesday, January 28, 1992

I'm better today. I'm taking antibiotics, so I'll be OK. Now Boris is sick too, and Oga says her throat hurts. I didn't tell you that Svjetlana brought us the flu from Sarajevo. She went to the dentist's, "picked up" the flu and took it away with her. And now here she is on Jahorina. She got sick first, then me, and now Boris, maybe even Oga. So the flu has cut short our fun. That's not very nice of it.

Sunday, February 2, 1992

We came back from Jahorina yesterday. I'm fine, but now Mommy is sick. She has a temperature and a cough. Daddy has a temperature too. I just have a cough. It's an epidemic.

Tuesday, February 4, 1992

School has started. Responsibilities ... I've just come back from music school. Well, it was OK, I guess.

I didn't tell you, dear Diary, that I have a notebook in which I paste fashion pictures. I have photos of Linda Evangelista, Claudia Schiffer, Cindy Crawford, Yasmine Le Bon.

Wednesday, February 15, 1992

Daddy's all right now, but Mommy's still sick. She just isn't getting better. It looks like she's got pneumonia. She's taken sick leave. She's going around seeing doctors.

I've got my responsibilities—school, music lessons, I study, practice the piano and pray to God that Mommy gets well and that we go to Jahorina. This miserable flu has ruined everything.

Thursday, March 5, 1992

Oh, God! Things are heating up in Sarajevo. On Sunday (March 1), a small group of armed civilians (as they say on TV) killed a Serbian wedding guest and wounded the priest. On March 2 (Monday) the whole city was full of barricades. There were "1,000" barricades. We didn't even have bread. At 6:00 people got fed up and went out into the streets. The procession set out from the cathedral. It went past the parliament building and made its way through the entire city. Several people were wounded at the Marshal Tito army barracks. People sang and cried "Bosnia, Bosnia," "Sarajevo, Sarajevo," "We'll live together" and "Come outside."

Zdravko Grebo[2] said on the radio that history was in the making.

At about 8:00 we heard the bell of a streetcar. The first streetcar had passed through town and life got back to normal. People poured out into the streets hoping that nothing like that would ever happen again. We joined the peace procession. When we got home we had a quiet night's sleep. The next day everything was the same as before. Classes, music school . . . But in the evening, the news came that 3,000 Chetniks [Serbian nationalists] were coming from Pale[3] to attack Sarajevo, and first, Baščaršija [the old part of town]. Melica said that new barricades had been put up in front of her house and that they wouldn't be sleeping at home tonight. They went to Uncle Nedjad's place. Later there was a real fight on YUTEL TV. Radovan Karadžič [Bosnian Serb leader] and Alija Izetbegovič [President of Bosnia-Herzegovina] phoned in and started arguing. Then Goran Milic[4] got angry and made them agree

---

[2] President of the Soros Foundation in Sarajevo and editor-in-chief of ZID, the independent radio station.

[3] Resort outside of Sarajevo, now headquarters of the Bosnian Serbs.

[4] A well-known newscaster on television, one of the founders of the YUTEL television station before the war.

to meet with some General Kukanjac.[5] Milič is great!!! Bravo!

On March 4 (Wednesday) the barricades were removed, the "kids" [a popular term for politicians] had come to some agreement. Great?!

That day our art teacher brought in a picture for our class-mistress (for March 8, Women's Day). We gave her the present, but she told us to go home. Something was wrong again! There was a panic. The girls started screaming and the boys quietly blinked their eyes. Daddy came home from work early that day too. But everything turned out OK. It's all too much!

Friday, March 6, 1992

Things are back to normal.

Tuesday, March 24, 1992

There's no more trouble in Sarajevo. But there is in other parts of B-H: Bosanski Brod, Derventa, Modriča. Terrible reports and pictures are coming in from all over. Mommy and Daddy won't let me

---

[5] General of the then Yugoslav Army, who was in Sarajevo when the war broke out.

watch TV when the news is on, but you can't hide all the bad things that are happening from us children. People are worried and sad again. The blue helmets (actually, they're blue berets) have arrived in Sarajevo. We're safer now. And the "kids" have retreated from the scene.

Daddy drove me to the building on the UN peace force command. He told me that now that the blue flag is flying in Sarajevo we can hope for something better.

Monday, March 30, 1992

Hey, Diary! You know what I think? Since Anne Frank called her diary Kitty, maybe I could give you a name too. What about:

ASFALTINA	PIDŽAMETA
ŠEFIKA	HIKMETA
ŠEVALA	MIMMY

or something else???

I'm thinking, thinking . . .

I've decided! I'm going to call you

MIMMY

All right, then, let's start.

Dear Mimmy,

It's almost half-term. We're all studying for our tests. Tomorrow we're supposed to go to a classical music concert at the Skenderija Hall. Our teacher says we shouldn't go because there will be 10,000 people, pardon me, children, there, and somebody might take us as hostages or plant a bomb in the concert hall. Mommy says I shouldn't go. So I won't.

Hey! You know who won the Yugovision Song Contest?! EXTRA NENA!!!???

I'm afraid to say this next thing. Melica says she heard at the hairdresser's that on Saturday, April 4, 1992, there's going to be BOOM—BOOM, BANG—BANG, CRASH Sarajevo. Translation: they're going to bomb Sarajevo.
Love,
Zlata

Friday, April 3, 1992

Dear Mimmy,
Mommy is at work. Daddy has gone to Zenica. I'm home from school and have been thinking. Azra leaves for Austria today. She's afraid of war. HEY! Still, I keep thinking about what Melica heard at the hairdresser's. What do I do if they bomb Sarajevo? Safia is here, and I'm listening to Radio-M. I feel safer.

Mommy says that what Melica heard at the hairdresser's is misinformation. I hope so!

Daddy came back from Zenica all upset. He says there are terrible crowds at the train and bus stations. People are leaving Sarajevo. Sad scenes. They're the people who believe the misinformation. Mothers and children are leaving, the fathers are staying behind, or just children are leaving, while their parents stay. Everybody is in tears. Daddy says he wishes he hadn't seen that.
Love you, Mimmy,
Zlata

Saturday, April 4, 1992
Today is Bairam [a Muslim religious holiday]. There aren't many people in the streets. I guess it's fear of the stories about Sarajevo being bombed. But there's no bombing. It looks as though Mommy was right when she said it was all misinformation. Thank God!
Love you,
Zlata

Sunday, April 5, 1992
Dear Mimmy,
I'm trying to concentrate so I can do my homework (reading), but I simply can't. Something is going on in town. You can hear gunfire from the hills.

Columns of people are spreading out from Dobrinja. They're trying to stop something, but they themselves don't know what. You can simply feel that something is coming, something very bad. On TV I see people in front of the B-H parliament building. The radio keeps playing the same song: "Sarajevo, My Love." That's all very nice, but my stomach is still in knots and I can't concentrate on my homework anymore.

Mimmy, I'm afraid of WAR!!!
Zlata

Monday, April 6, 1992

Dear Mimmy,

Yesterday the people in front of the parliament tried peacefully to cross the Vrbanja bridge. But they were shot at. Who? How? Why? A girl, a medical student from Dubrovnik, was KILLED. Her blood spilled onto the bridge. In her final moments all she said was: "Is this Sarajevo?" HORRIBLE, HORRIBLE HORRIBLE!

NO ONE AND NOTHING HERE IS NOR-MAL!

The Baščaršija has been destroyed! Those "fine gentlemen" from Pale fired on Baščaršija!

Since yesterday people have been inside the B-H parliament. Some of them are standing outside, in front of it. We've moved my television set into the living room, so I watch Channel I on one TV and "Good Vibrations" on the other. Now they're shooting from the Holiday Inn, killing people in front of the parliament. And Bokica is there with Vanja and Andrej. Oh, God!

Maybe we'll go to the cellar. You, Mimmy, will go with me, of course. I'm desperate. The people in front of the parliament are desperate too. Mimmy, war is here. PEACE, NOW!

They say they're going to attack RTV Sarajevo [radio and TV center]. But they haven't. They've stopped shooting in our neighborhood. KNOCK! KNOCK! (I'm knocking on wood for good luck.)

WHEW! It was tough. Oh, God! They're shooting again!!!
Zlata

Thursday, April 9, 1992

Dear Mimmy,

I'm not going to school. All the schools in Sarajevo are closed. There's danger hiding in these hills above Sarajevo. But I think things are slowly calming down. The heavy shelling and explosions have stopped. There's occasional gunfire, but it quickly falls silent. Mommy and Daddy aren't going to work. They're buying food in huge quantities. Just in case, I guess. God forbid!

Still, it's very tense. Mommy is beside herself, Daddy tries to calm her down. Mommy has long conversations on the phone. She calls, other people call, the phone is in constant use.
Zlata

Sunday, April 12, 1992

Dear Mimmy,

The new sections of town—Dobrinja, Mojmilo, Vojničko polje—are being badly shelled. Everything is being destroyed, burned, the people are in shelters. Here in the middle of town, where we live, it's different. It's quiet. People go out. It was a nice warm spring day today. We went out too. Vaso Miškin Street was full of people, children. It looked like a peace march. People came out to be together, they don't want war. They want to live and enjoy themselves the way they used to. That's only natural, isn't it? Who likes or wants war, when it's the worst thing in the world?

I keep thinking about the march I joined today. It's bigger and stronger than war. That's why it will win. The people must be the ones to win, not the war, because war has nothing to do with humanity. War is something inhuman.
Zlata

Tuesday, April 14, 1992

Dear Mimmy,
People are leaving Sarajevo. The airport, train and bus stations are packed. I saw sad pictures on TV of people parting. Families, friends separating. Some are leaving, others staying. It's so sad. Why? These people and children aren't guilty of anything. Keka and Braco came early this morning. They're in the kitchen with Mommy and Daddy, whispering. Keka and Mommy are crying. I don't think they know what to do—whether to stay or to go. Neither way is good.
Zlata

Wednesday, April 15, 1992

Dear Mimmy,
There has been terrible gunfire in Mojmilo [a part of Sarajevo]. Mirna spent a whole forty-eight hours

in the shelter. I talked to her on the phone, but not for long because she had to go back down to the shelter. I feel sorry for her.

Bojana and Verica are going to England. Oga is going to Italy. And worst of all, Martina and Matea have already left. They went to Ohrid [a lakeside town in Macedonia]. Keka is crying, Braco is crying and Mommy is crying. She's on the phone right now, and she's crying. And "those boys" up there in the hills keep shooting at us. I just heard that Dejan has left too.

OOOHHHHH! Why war?!
Love you, Mimmy,
Zlata

Thursday, April 16, 1992

Dear Mimmy,
Martina, Matea and Dejan didn't leave, after all. That's really not fair! Yes, of course it is, they mustn't go. But it isn't fair because we all cried our eyes out and in the end they didn't leave. There are not enough buses, trains or planes for all the people who want to get out of here.
Love you,
Zlata

Dear Mimmy,

There's shooting, shells are falling. This really is WAR. Mommy and Daddy are worried, they sit up until late at night, talking. They're wondering what to do, but it's hard to know. Whether to leave and split up, or stay here together. Keka wants to take me to Ohrid. Mommy can't make up her mind— she's constantly in tears. She tries to hide it from me, but I see everything. I see that things aren't good here. There's no peace. War has suddenly entered our town, our homes, our thoughts, our lives. It's terrible.

It's also terrible that Mommy has packed my suitcase.

Love,
Zlata

Monday, April 20, 1992

Dear Mimmy,

War is no joke, it seems. It destroys, kills, burns, separates, brings unhappiness. Terrible shells fell today on Baščaršija, the old town center. Terrible explosions. We went down into the cellar, the cold, dark, revolting cellar. And ours isn't even all that safe.

Mommy, Daddy and I just stood there, holding on to one another in a corner that looked safe. Standing there in the dark, in the warmth of my parents' arms, I thought about leaving Sarajevo. Everybody is thinking about it, and so am I. I couldn't bear to go alone, to leave behind Mommy and Daddy, Grandma and Granddad. And going with just Mommy isn't any good either. The best would be for all three of us to go. But Daddy can't. So I've decided we should stay here together. Tomorrow I'll tell Keka that you have to be brave and stay with those you love and those who love you. I can't leave my parents, and I don't like the other idea of leaving my father behind alone either.
Your Zlata

Tuesday, April 21, 1992

Dear Mimmy,

It's horrible in Sarajevo today. Shells falling, people and children getting killed, shooting. We will probably spend the night in the cellar. Since ours isn't safe, we're going to our neighbors', the Bobars' house. The Bobar family consists of Grandma Mira, Auntie Boda, Uncle Žika (her husband), Maja and Bojana. When the shooting gets bad, Žika phones us and then we run across the yard, over the ladder

and the table, into their building and finally knock
at their door. Until just the other day we took the
street, but there's shooting and it's not safe anymore. I'm getting ready to go to the cellar. I've
packed my backpack with biscuits, juice, a deck of
cards and a few other "things." I can still hear the
cannon fire, and something that sounds like it.
Love you, Mimmy,
Zlata

Wednesday, April 22, 1992

Dear Mimmy,
We spent the whole night in the Bobars' cellar. We
went there at around 9:30 and came home at
about 10:30 the next morning. I slept from 4:00 to
9:30 A.M. It boomed and shook really badly last night.
Zlata

Sunday, April 26, 1992

Dear Mimmy,
We spent Thursday night with the Bobars again.
The next day we had no electricity. We had no
bread, so for the first time in her life Mommy baked
some. She was scared how it would turn out. It
turned out like bread—good bread. That was the

day I was supposed to go to Ohrid with M&M. But I didn't, and neither did they.
Ciao!
Your Zlata

Tuesday, April 28, 1992

Dear Mimmy,
SNIFFLE! Martina, SNIFFLE, and Matea, SNIFFLE, left YESTERDAAAY! They left by bus for Krško [a town in Slovenia]. They went with Keka. Oga has gone too, so has Dejan, Mirna will be leaving tomorrow or the next day, and soon Marijana will be going too.
SNIFFLE!
Everybody has gone. I'm left with no friends.
Zlata

Wednesday, April 29, 1992

Dear Mimmy,
I'd write to you much more about the war if only I could. But I simply don't want to remember all these horrible things. They make me sick. Please, don't be mad at me. I'll write something.
I love you,
Zlata

Dear Mimmy,

Today was truly, absolutely the worst day ever in Sarajevo. The shooting started around noon. Mommy and I moved into the hall. Daddy was in his office, under our apartment, at the time. We told him on the intercom to run quickly to the downstairs lobby where we'd meet him. We brought Cicko [Zlata's canary] with us. The gunfire was getting worse, and we couldn't get over the wall to the Bobars', so we ran down to our own cellar.

The cellar is ugly, dark, smelly. Mommy, who's terrified of mice, had two fears to cope with. The three of us were in the same corner as the other day. We listened to the pounding shells, the shooting, the thundering noise overhead. We even heard planes. At one moment I realized that this awful cellar was the only place that could save our lives. Suddenly, it started to look almost warm and nice. It was the only way we could defend ourselves against all this terrible shooting. We heard glass shattering in our street. Horrible. I put my fingers in my ears to block out the terrible sounds. I was worried about Cicko. We had left him behind in the lobby. Would he catch cold there? Would something hit him? I was terribly hungry and thirsty. We had left our half-cooked lunch in the kitchen.

When the shooting died down a bit, Daddy ran over to our apartment and brought us back some sandwiches. He said he could smell something burning and that the phones weren't working. He brought our TV set down to the cellar. That's when we learned that the main post office (near us) was on fire and that they had kidnapped our President. At around 8:00 we went back up to our apartment. Almost every window in our street was broken. Ours were all right, thank God. I saw the post office in flames. A terrible sight. The fire-fighters battled with the raging fire. Daddy took a few photos of the post office being devoured by the flames. He said they wouldn't come out because I had been fiddling with something on the camera. I was sorry. The whole apartment smelled of the burning fire. God, and I used to pass by there every day. It had just been done up. It was huge and beautiful, and now it was being swallowed up by the flames. It was disappearing. That's what this neighborhood of mine looks like, my Mimmy. I wonder what it's like in other parts of town? I heard on the radio that it was awful around the Eternal Flame. The place is knee-deep in glass. We're worried about Grandma and Granddad. They live there. Tomorrow, if we can go out, we'll see how they are. A terrible day.

This has been the worst, most awful day in my eleven-year-old life. I hope it will be the only one. Mommy and Daddy are very edgy. I have to go to bed.

Ciao!

Zlata

Dear Mimmy,

Daddy managed to run across the bridge over the Miljacka and get to Grandma and Granddad. He came running back, all upset, sweating with fear and sadness. They're all right, thank God. Tito Street looks awful. The heavy shelling has destroyed shop windows, cars, apartments, the fronts and roofs of buildings. Luckily, not too many people were hurt because they managed to take shelter. Neda (Mommy's girlfriend) rushed over to see how we were and to tell us that they were OK and hadn't had any damage. But it was terrible.

We talked through the window with Auntie Boda and Bojana just now. They were in the street yesterday when that heavy shooting broke out. They managed to get to Stela's cellar.

Zlata

Dear Mimmy,

The shooting seems to be dying down. I guess they've caused enough misery, although I don't know why. It has something to do with politics. I just hope the "kids" come to some agreement. Oh, if only they would, so we could live and breathe as human beings again. The things that have happened here these past few days are terrible. I want it to stop forever. PEACE! PEACE!

I didn't tell you, Mimmy, that we've rearranged things in the apartment. My room and Mommy and Daddy's are too dangerous to be in. They face the hills, which is where they're shooting from. If only you knew how scared I am to go near the windows and into those rooms. So, we turned a safe corner of the sitting room into a "bedroom." We sleep on mattresses on the floor. It's strange and awful. But, it's safer that way. We've turned everything around for safety. We put Cicko in the kitchen. He's safe there, although once the shooting starts there's nowhere safe except the cellar. I suppose all this will stop and we'll all go back to our usual places.
Ciao!
Zlata

Dear Mimmy,

I was almost positive the war would stop, but today . . . Today a shell fell on the park in front of my house, the park where I used to play and sit with my girlfriends. A lot of people were hurt. From what I hear Jaca, Jaca's mother, Selma, Nina, our neighbor Dado and who knows how many other people who happened to be there were wounded. Dado, Jaca and her mother have come home from the hospital, Selma lost a kidney but I don't know how she is, because she's still in the hospital. AND NINA IS DEAD. A piece of shrapnel lodged in her brain and she died. She was such a sweet, nice little girl. We went to kindergarten together, and we used to play together in the park. Is it possible I'll never see Nina again? Nina, an innocent eleven-year-old little girl—the victim of a stupid war. I feel sad. I cry and wonder why? She didn't do anything. A disgusting war has destroyed a young child's life. Nina, I'll always remember you as a wonderful little girl.

Love, Mimmy,

Zlata

Dear Mimmy,

Life goes on. The past is cruel, and that's exactly why we should forget it.

The present is cruel too and I can't forget it. There's no joking with war. My present reality is the cellar, fear, shells, fire.

Terrible shooting broke out the night before last. We were afraid that we might be hit by shrapnel or a bullet, so we ran over to the Bobars'. We spent all of that night, the next day and the next night in the cellar and in Nedo's apartment. (Nedo is a refugee from Grbavica. He left his parents and came here to his sister's empty apartment.) We saw terrible scenes on TV. The town in ruins, burning, people and children being killed. It's unbelievable.

The phones aren't working, we haven't been able to find out anything about Grandma and Granddad, Melica, how people in other parts of town are doing. On TV we saw the place where Mommy works, Vodoprivreda, all in flames. It's on the aggressor's side of town (Grbavica). Mommy cried. She's depressed. All her years of work and effort—up in flames. It's really horrible. All around Vodoprivreda there were cars burning, people dying, and nobody could help them. God, why is this happening?

I'M SO MAD I WANT TO SCREAM AND BREAK EVERYTHING!

Your Zlata

Dear Mimmy,

The shelling here has stopped. Daddy managed to run over to Grandma and Granddad's to see how they are, how they've been coping with the madness of the past few days. They're all right, thank God. Melica and her family are all right, and Grandma heard from Vinko that Meda and Bojan (an aunt and her son) are also all right.

The situation at the Marshal Tito barracks and in the new parts of town is terrible. It's a madhouse around the electricity board building and the radio and television center. I can't watch television anymore. I can't bear to. The area around Otes seems to be the only place that is still quiet. Mommy's brother Braco and his family live there. They're so lucky, there's no shooting where they live.

Zlata

Sunday, May 17, 1992

Dear Mimmy,

It's now definite: there's no more school. The war

has interrupted our lessons, closed down the schools, sent children to cellars instead of classrooms. They'll give us the grades we got at the end of last term. So I'll get a report card saying I've finished fifth grade.

Ciao!

Zlata

Wednesday, May 20, 1992

Dear Mimmy,

The shooting has died down. Today Mommy felt brave enough to cross the bridge. She saw Grandma and Granddad, ran into various people she knows and heard a lot of sad news. She came back all miserable. Her brother was wounded on May 14, driving home from work. Her brother is hurt and she doesn't find out about it until today—that's terrible. He was wounded in the leg and is in the hospital. How can she get to him? It's like being at the other end of the world now. They told her he's all right, but she doesn't believe them and keeps crying. If only the shooting would stop, she could go to the hospital. She says: "I won't believe it until I see him with my own eyes."

Zlata

Spring 1991. Zlata is in the fifth grade enjoying school before the bombs start falling on Sarajevo.

War breaks out in Sarajevo. In the beginning, the arrival of the blue berets brought hope.

Cooking is quite an achievement without electricity.
It is sometimes necessary to search the neighborhood
to find an oven. Zlata's mother proudly shows
off the bread she made in a pressure cooker.

Thursday, May 21, 1992

Dear Mimmy,

Mommy went to see Braco in the hospital today. He's alive. That's the most important thing. But he's badly wounded. It's his knee. Two hundred wounded were brought to the clinic that day. They were going to amputate his leg, but his friend Dr. Adnan Dizdar (the surgeon) recognized him, canceled the amputation and took him into the operating room. The operation lasted four-and-a-half hours and the doctors say it was a success. But he'll have to stay in bed for a long, long time. He has some rods, a cast, all sorts of things on his leg. Mommy is terribly worried and sad. So are Grandma and Granddad (that's what Mommy tells me, because I haven't seen them since April 12; I haven't been out of the house). In the end he was lucky. I hope it will turn out all right. Hold on there, Braco!!!
Your Zlata

Saturday, May 23, 1992

Dear Mimmy,

I'm not writing to you about me anymore. I'm writing to you about war, death, injuries, shells, sadness and sorrow. Almost all my friends have left. Even if they were here, who knows whether we'd be able to see one another. The phones aren't working, we couldn't even talk to one another. Vanja and Andrej have gone to join Srdjan in Dubrovnik. The war has stopped there. They're lucky. I was so unhappy because of that war in Dubrovnik. I never dreamed it would move to Sarajevo. Verica and Bojana have also left.

I now spend all my time with Bojana and Maja. They're my best friends now. Bojana is a year-and-a-half older than me, she's finished seventh grade and we have a lot in common. Maja is in her last year of school. She's much older than I am, but she's wonderful. I'm lucky to have them, otherwise I'd be all alone among the grown-ups.

On the news they reported the death of Silva Rizvanbegović, a doctor at the Emergency Clinic, who's Mommy's friend. She was in an ambulance. They were driving a wounded man to get him help. Lots of people Mommy and Daddy know have been killed. Oh, God, what is happening here???

Love,
Zlata

Dear Mimmy,

Today the Zetra Hall, the Olympic Zetra, went up in flames. The whole world knew about it, it was the Olympic beauty, and now it's going up in flames. The firefighters tried to save it, and our Žika joined them. But it didn't stand a chance. The forces of war don't know anything about love and the desire to save something. They just know how to destroy, burn, take things away. So they wanted Zetra to disappear as well. It makes me sad, Mimmy.

I feel as though no one and nothing here will survive.

Your Zlata

Tuesday, May 26, 1992

Dear Mimmy,

I keep thinking about Mirna; May 13 was her birthday. I would love to see her so much. I keep asking Mommy and Daddy to take me to her. She left Mojmilo with her mother and father to go to her grandparents' place. Their apartment was shelled and they had to leave it.

There's no shooting, the past few days have been quiet. I asked Daddy to take me to Mirna's because

I made her a little birthday present. I miss her. I wish I could see her.

I was such a nag that Daddy decided to take me to her. We went there, but the downstairs door was locked. We couldn't call out to them and I came home feeling disappointed. The present is waiting for her, so am I. I suppose we'll see each other.
Love,
Zlata

Wednesday, May 27, 1992

Dear Mimmy,
SLAUGHTER! MASSACRE! HORROR! CRIME! BLOOD! SCREAMS! TEARS! DESPAIR!

That's what Vaso Miškin Street looks like today. Two shells exploded in the street and one in the market. Mommy was nearby at the time. She ran to Grandma and Granddad's. Daddy and I were beside ourselves because she hadn't come home. I saw some of it on TV but I still can't believe what I actually saw. It's unbelievable. I've got a lump in my throat and a knot in my tummy. HORRIBLE. They're taking the wounded to the hospital. It's a madhouse. We kept going to the window hoping to see Mommy, but she wasn't back. They released a list of the dead and wounded. Daddy and I were tearing our hair out. We didn't know what had happened to her. Was she alive? At 4:00, Daddy decided to go and check the hospital. He got dressed, and I got ready to go to the Bobars', so as not to stay at home alone. I looked out the window one more time and . . . I SAW MOMMY RUNNING ACROSS THE BRIDGE. As she came into the house she started shaking and crying. Through her tears she told us how she had seen dismembered bodies. All the neighbors came because they had been afraid for her. Thank God, Mommy is with us. Thank God.

A HORRIBLE DAY. UNFORGETTABLE.

HORRIBLE! HORRIBLE!

Your Zlata

Thursday, May 28, 1992

Dear Mimmy,

It started at around 10:00. First we went to Neda's. I put Saša to sleep and left the bedroom. I looked toward the bathroom, and then . . . BOOM. The window in the bathroom shattered into pieces and I was alone in the hall and saw it all. I began to cry hysterically. Then we went down into the cellar. When things calmed down we went up to Neda's

and spent the night there. Today in Vaso Miškin Street people signed the book of mourning and laid flowers. They renamed the street and now it's called the Street of Anti-Fascist Resistance.
Zlata

Friday, May 29, 1992

Dear Mimmy,
I'm at Neda's. The result of last night's fascism is broken glass in Daddy's office and at the Bobars' shattered windows. A shell fell on the house across the way, and I can't even tell you how many fell nearby. The whole town was in flames.
Your Zlata

Saturday, May 30, 1992

Dear Mimmy,
The City Maternity Hospital has burned down. I was born there. Hundreds of thousands of new babies, new residents of Sarajevo, won't have the luck to be born in this maternity hospital now. It was new. The fire devoured everything. The mothers and babies were saved. When the fire broke out two women were giving birth. The babies are alive. God, people get killed here, they die here, they disappear, things

go up in flames here, and out of the flames, new lives are born.

Your Zlata

Dear Mimmy,

Today is Maja's birthday. She's eighteen. She's an adult now. She's a grown-up. It's an important day in her life, but, what can you do, she's celebrating it in wartime. We all did our best to make this day special for her, but she was sad and moody. Why did this war have to ruin everything for her? Maja isn't even having her senior prom, or an evening gown. All there is here is war, war and more war.

Fortunately, there wasn't too much shooting, so we could sit in peace. Auntie Boda made a special lunch (how special can it be in wartime???). Mommy used the last walnuts in the house to make a cake (Maja and her eighteen years deserve it). We gave her a necklace and bracelet made of Ohrid pearls. She got a lot of valuable presents made of gold. Well, you're only eighteen once in your life. Happy birthday to you Maja on this big day, may all your other birthdays be celebrated in peace.

Zlata

Dear Mimmy,

There's been no electricity for quite some time and we keep thinking about the food in the freezer. There's not much left as it is. It would be a pity for all of it to go bad. There's meat and vegetables and fruit. How can we save it?

Daddy found an old wood-burning stove in the attic. It's so old it looks funny. In the cellar we found some wood, put the stove outside in the yard, lit it and are trying to save the food from the refrigerator. We cooked everything, and joining forces with the Bobars, enjoyed ourselves. There was veal and chicken, squid, cherry strudel, meat and potato pies. All sorts of things. It's a pity, though, that we had to eat everything so quickly. We even overate. WE HAD A MEAT STROKE.

We washed down our refrigerators and freezers. Who knows when we'll be able to cook like this again. Food is becoming a big problem in Sarajevo. There's nothing to buy, and even cigarettes and coffee are becoming a problem for grown-ups. The last reserves are being used up. God, are we going to go hungry to boot???

Zlata

Dear Mimmy,

At about eleven o'clock last night it started to thunder again. No, not the weather, the shells. We ran over to Nedo's. I fell asleep there, but Mommy and Daddy went back home.

There's no electricity. We're cooking on the wood stove in the yard. Everybody is. The whole neighborhood. What luck to have this old stove.

Daddy and Žika keep fiddling with the radio, listening to the news. They found RFI (Radio France Internationale) in our language. That's at nine o'clock in the evening and they listen to it regularly. Bojana and I usually play cards, word games or draw something.

Love,

Zlata

Dear Mimmy,

There's still no electricity, so we're still cooking on the stove in the yard. Around 2:00, when we were doing something around the stove, a shell fell on the opposite corner of the street, destroying Zoka's wonderful jewelry shop. We ran straight to the cellar, waiting for the barrage. Luckily there was only that one shell, so we went back at around 4:00.

Your Zlata

Tuesday, June 16, 1992

Dear Mimmy,

Our windows are broken. All of them except the ones in my room. That's the result of the revolting shell that fell again on Zoka's jewelry shop, across the way from us. I was alone in the house at the time. Mommy and Daddy were down in the yard, getting lunch ready, and I had gone upstairs to set the table. Suddenly I heard a terrible bang and glass breaking. I was terrified and ran toward the hall. That same moment, Mommy and Daddy were at the door. Out of breath, worried, sweating and pale they hugged me and we ran to the cellar, because the shells usually come one after the other. When I realized what had happened, I started to cry and shake. Everybody tried to calm me down, but I was very upset. I barely managed to pull myself together.

We returned to the apartment to find the rooms full of glass and the windows broken. We cleared away the glass and put plastic sheeting over the windows. We had had a close shave with that shell and

60

shrapnel. I picked up a piece of shrapnel and the tail end of a grenade, put them in a box and thanked God I had been in the kitchen, because I could have been hit . . . HORRIBLE! I don't know how often I've written that word. HORRIBLE. We've had too much horror. The days here are full of horror. Maybe we in Sarajevo could rename the day and call it horror, because that's really what it's like.

Love,
Zlata

Thursday, June 18, 1992

Dear Mimmy,

Today we heard some more sad, sad news. Our country house in Crnotina, a tower that's about 150 years old, has burned down. Like the post office, it disappeared in the flames. I loved it so much. We spent last summer there. I had a wonderful time. I always looked forward to going there. We had redone it so nicely, bought new furniture, new rugs, put in new windows, given it all our love and warmth, and its beauty was our reward. It lived through so many wars, so many years and now it's gone. It has burned down to the ground. Our neighbors Žiga, Meho and Bečir were killed. That's even sadder. Vildana's house also burned down. All the houses burned down. Lots of people were killed. It's terribly sad news.

I keep asking why? What for? Who's to blame? I ask, but there's no answer. All I know is that we are living in misery. Yes, I know, politics is to blame for it all. I said I wasn't interested in politics, but in order to find out the answer I have to know something about it. They tell me only a few things. I'll probably find out and understand much more one day. Mommy and Daddy don't discuss politics with me. They probably think I'm too young or maybe they themselves don't know anything. They just keep telling me: This will pass—"it has to pass"????????
Your Zlata

Saturday, June 20, 1992

Dear Mimmy,
Auntie Radmila (Mommy's friend from work) came today. She came from Vojničko polje (a new housing complex). Her apartment has been completely destroyed. Wiped out in the shelling. Everything in it has been destroyed. All that's left is a useless pile of furniture, clothes, pictures and all the other

things that go into an apartment. She's sad, because her daughters Sunčica and Mirna aren't there (they're in Zagreb), but she's glad they didn't have to live through the hell of Vojničko polje. Today we heard that Narmin Tulič, the actor at the Experimental Theater, lost both his legs. Awful! Awful! Awful!

Saša went to stay with his grandmother. But he'll probably be coming back.

Your Zlata

Monday, June 22, 1992

Dear Mimmy,

More blood on the streets of Sarajevo. Another massacre. In Tito Street. Three people killed, thirty-five wounded. Shells fell on Radič, Miss Irbin and Šenoa streets. About fifteen people were killed in the three streets. I'm worried that something may have happened to Marina's, Marijana's or Ivana's parents.

These people just go on killing. MURDERS!

I pity them for being so very, very stupid, so servile, for humiliating themselves so much in front of certain people. Terrible!!!!!!

Your Zlata

Tuesday, June 23, 1992

Dear Mimmy,

Cicko could have been killed today. He fell out of the kitchen window onto a tin roof. We ran downstairs into the yard and brought him in. He just lay there in the corner of his cage, blinking madly. I tried to cheer him up with a leaf of lettuce. Fortunately he survived.

A shell fell on the central market and the cathedral today.

The electricity went out at eight o'clock last night. It's now 11:30 and it's still not back.
HORRIBLE
Zlata

Wednesday, June 24, 1992

Dear Mimmy,

9:45—the water is back on. Still no electricity. 10:30—we've still got water. 12:00—no water, but we've got electricity.
YESSS!

Mimmy, I've just realized that all my friends have left: Oga, Martina, Matea, Dejan, Vanja and Andrej.
OHHHH!

They're shooting outside. Bojana and I aren't allowed to go out into the yard, so we're rollerskating in the lobby of their building. It's not bad!

These are the books I've read so far: *Mommy I Love You, Eagles Fly Early,* and the next book I'm going to read is *Little Toto.*

Your Zlata

Dear Mimmy,

BOREDOM!!! SHOOTING!!! SHELLING!!! PEOPLE BEING KILLED!!! DESPAIR!!! HUNGER!!! MISERY!!! FEAR!!!

That's my life! The life of an innocent eleven-year-old schoolgirl!! A schoolgirl without a school, without the fun and excitement of school. A child without games, without friends, without the sun, without birds, without nature, without fruit, without chocolate or sweets, with just a little powdered milk. In short, a child without a childhood. A wartime child. I now realize that I am really living through a war, I am witnessing an ugly, disgusting war. I and thousands of other children in this town that is being destroyed, that is crying, weeping, seeking help, but getting none. God, will this ever stop, will I ever be a schoolgirl again, will I ever enjoy my childhood

again? I once heard that childhood is the most wonderful time of your life. And it is. I loved it, and now an ugly war is taking it all away from me. Why? I feel sad. I feel like crying. I am crying.
Your Zlata

Thursday, July 2, 1992

Dear Mimmy,
We gave ourselves a treat today. We picked the cherries off the tree in the yard and ate them all up. We had watched it blossom and its small green fruits slowly turn red and now here we were eating them. Oh, you're a wonderful cherry tree! The plum tree hasn't gotten any fruit so we won't even get to try it! I miss fruit a lot. In these days of war in Sarajevo, there is no basic food or any of the other things a person needs, and there is no fruit. But now I can say that I ate myself silly on cherries.

Braco, Mommy's brother, is getting better. He's even walking a bit now.
Zlata

Friday, July 3, 1992

Dear Mimmy,
Mommy goes to work at her new office. She goes if

there's no shooting, but we never know when the shelling will start. It's dangerous to walk around town. It's especially dangerous to cross our bridge, because snipers shoot at you. You have to run across. Every time she goes out, Daddy and I go to the window to watch her run. Mommy says: "I didn't know the Miljacka (our river) was so wide. You run, and you run, and you run, and there's no end to the bridge." That's fear, Mimmy, fear that you'll be hit by something.

Daddy doesn't go to work. The two of us stay at home, waiting for Mommy. When the sirens go off we worry about how and when and if she'll get home. Oh, the relief when she walks in!

Neda came for lunch today. Afterward we played cards. Neda said something about going to Zagreb. It made Mommy sad, because they've been friends since childhood. They grew up together, spent their whole lives together. I was sad too because I love her and I know she loves me.

Zlata

Sunday, July 5, 1992

Dear Mimmy,

I don't remember when I last left the house. It must be almost two months ago now. I really miss Grandma and Granddad. I used to go there every day, and now I haven't seen them for such a long time.

I spend my days in the house and in the cellar. That's my wartime childhood. And it's summer. Other children are vacationing on the seaside, in the mountains, swimming, sunbathing, enjoying themselves. God, what did I do to deserve being in a war, spending my days in a way that no child should. I feel caged. All I can see through the broken windows is the park in front of my house. Empty, deserted, no children, no joy. I hear the sound of shells, and everything around me smells of war. War is now my life. OOHHH, I can't stand it anymore! I want to scream and cry. I wish I could play the piano at least, but I can't even do that because it's in "the dangerous room," where I'm not allowed. How long is this going to go on???
Zlata

Tuesday, July 7, 1992

Dear Mimmy,
There was no water yesterday, the day before or the day before that. It came at around 8:30 this morning and now, at 10:30, it's slowly disappearing again.

We filled whatever we could find with water and

now have to save on the precious liquid. You have to save on everything in this war, including water and food.

Mommy is at work, Daddy is reading something and I'm going to Bojana's because there's no shooting.

Saturday, July 11, 1992

Dear Mimmy,
Nedo brought us a little visitor today. A kitten. It followed him and he couldn't just leave it in the street so he picked it up and brought it home. We'll call it Skinny, Lanky, Kitty, Mikana, Persa, Cici . . . ???? It's orange, has white socks and a white patch on its chest. It's cute, but a little wild.
Zlata

Tuesday, July 14, 1992

Dear Mimmy,
On July 8 we got a UN package. Humanitarian aid. Inside were 6 cans of beef, 5 cans of fish, 2 boxes of cheese, 3 kilos of detergent, 5 bars of soap, 2 kilos of sugar and 5 liters of cooking oil. All in all, a super package. But Daddy had to stand in line for four hours to get it.

Dobrinja has been liberated. They received UN packages there too.

We're waiting to hear what the Security Council has decided about military intervention in B-H.

The water and electricity went off the day before yesterday, July 12, and still aren't back.

Ciao!
Zlata

Friday, July 17, 1992

Dear Mimmy,

We named the kitten Cici. Nedo gave it a bath, we feed it milk and biscuits, even rice. She has to get used to wartime food like the rest of us! She's cute. She has a beautiful head. We've all fallen in love with her and she is slowly getting used to us. Bojana and I hold her in our lap, stroke her and she purrs. That means she likes it, she's happy. She must be lucky. Who knows whether she'd still be alive. She could have been hit by shrapnel, or died of hunger or been attacked by a stray dog. Nedo really did a good deed there. So, now we have a new member in this family we call THE NEIGHBORHOOD.

Ciao!
Zlata

Dear Mimmy,

I forgot to tell you that a few days ago two girls moved into the apartment next door. They're called Emina and Samra. They're super. Emina is like Mommy, they like the same colors, they like clothes and both, I have to say, are panicky. Samra is a refugee from Grbavica and she left everything behind. She's taking it all pretty well. Her mother died a few years ago, maybe that's why she's strong and can put up with all this more easily. Emina's sister is married to Samra's brother. Their names are Alma and Kemo. They have an eight-year-old boy named Haris and a two-and-a-half-year-old little girl named Nejra. Samra and Emina talk about Nejra all the time, how cute and talkative she is. I'd really like to meet her.

Ciao!

Zlata

Monday, July 20, 1992

Dear Mimmy,

Since I'm in the house all the time, I watch the world through the window. Just a piece of the world.

There are lots of beautiful pedigree dogs roaming the streets. Their owners probably had to let them go because they couldn't feed them anymore. Sad. Yesterday I watched a cocker spaniel cross the bridge, not knowing which way to go. He was lost. He wanted to go forward, but then he stopped, turned around and looked back. He was probably looking for his master. Who knows whether his master is still alive? Even animals suffer here. Even they aren't spared by the war.

Ciao!

Zlata

Sunday, July 26, 1992

Dear Mimmy,

Braco Lajtner was here yesterday. He brought us letters from Keka, Martina and Matea. They're really unhappy at being separated from Braco, and we all cried when we read the letters. Even Daddy. Wartime life is hard, but so is refugee life.

Martina and Matea have made some new friends, and Martina went to the Guns 'n' Roses concert in Budapest.

So far I've read the following books: *Mommy I Love You, Little Toto, Ringo Starr, The Twilight of the*

Geniuses, Hajduk in Belgrade, Follow Me, The Secret Diary of Adrian Mole. Nice!

Braco, Mommy's brother, has left the hospital and is staying with Grandma and Granddad. He feels much better, both physically and mentally.

The neighborhood community center is organizing a summer school. I've signed up for English, computer studies and music, but Bojana is just taking computer studies.

Mommy saw Mislo, Mirna's daddy today. He says they're all right, that Mirna is spending her time the same as me. If only we could see each other.

The Security Council is hopeless. It makes no reasonable decisions at all.

Your Zlata

Wednesday, July 29, 1992

Dear Mimmy,

Mommy came home from work in tears today. She had very, very sad news. Mladjo (Srdjan's brother) was killed in front of his house yesterday. The funeral was today, she read it in the papers, but it was too late. Awful. What's happening here is unbelievable. People are getting killed, disappearing, being buried, and their closest friends can't even attend the funeral. Only Seka (Bokica's sister) was there. Srdjan and his parents are in Dubrovnik, and Mladjo's wife and three children, Maja, Bojana and Nebojša, are in Montenegro. They don't even know that he's dead. And who knows when they'll hear the sad news, because Sarajevo is cut off from the rest of the world. The phones aren't working. God, what is happening?

Bojana, Maja and Nebojša have lost their daddy. A disgusting war has taken their daddy from them. Sad, awfully sad. Mladjo was a wonderful man.
Love,
Zlata

Tuesday, August 4, 1992

Dear Mimmy,

Five months. Five months of brutal aggression against the independent, sovereign state of Bosnia and Herzegovina.

A bullet entered the Bobars' sitting room. It shattered the window, broke the TV antenna and part of the glass table, went through the armchair, broke the glass on the door, and finally FELL! The Bobars have had three other bullets. One tore through the plastic and lodged sideways in the wardrobe where it grazed Auntie Boda's university degree and, finally, FELL! Another one broke through a window and lodged in the wall. And the third ripped through the plastic, grazed the armchair, entered Auntie Boda's closet where it tore her vest and then again—FELL!

Wednesday, August 5, 1992

Dear Mimmy,

Another sad piece of news in the paper. Mommy found out that her uncle (Uncle Halim) has died. He was old but this war speeded up his death. I'm so sorry. He was a wonderful old man. I loved him. That's how it is in wartime, Mimmy. Your loved ones die and you don't even know about it. War doesn't let you stay in touch with people, except for your neighbors. The neighborhood is our life now. Everything happens within that circle, it's the circle you know, everything else is remote.

Zlata

Friday, August 7, 1992

Dear Mimmy,

It thundered here today. I don't know how many shells fell nearby. It was quiet when Daddy went with Samra to get the aid package. But then the shelling suddenly started. An explosion. It thundered. Emina was at our place. There was a terrible boom. Glass shattered, bricks fell, there were clouds of dust. We didn't know where to run. We were convinced that the shell had fallen on our roof. We were on our way to the cellar when we heard Nedo frantically calling out to us, running toward us through the dust, bricks and broken glass. We ran over to the Bobars' cellar. They were all down there. We were shaking. Mommy most of all. In tears, she asked about Daddy, whether he had come back. When we calmed down a bit they told us that a shell had fallen on the roof of Emina's house, above her apartment. We were lucky, because that's only about ten meters away from the roof over our apartment. Everything turned out OK. Daddy and Samra soon came running in. They had been worried about us too. When we got back to the apartment it was full of dust, pieces of brick, and we found a piece of shrapnel in the bathroom. We rolled up our sleeves and started cleaning the place up. I was scared it would start again. Luckily, it didn't. Another horrible day.

Your Zlata

Monday, August 10, 1992

Dear Mimmy,
Mommy's Braco is fine. He's already walking well. Today he went to Otes. He'll be working in the press center there, reporting on the situation. Things are all right there. They have no shooting and they have food. They're lucky. I really miss my cousins Mikica and Dačo. I haven't seen them since the war broke out.
Your Zlata

Tuesday, August 11, 1992

Dear Mimmy,
Shelling, killing, darkness and hunger continue in Sarajevo. Sad!

I still don't go out. I play with Bojana and with my kitty Cici. Cici has brightened up this misery of a life. How you can come to love an animal! She doesn't talk, but she speaks with her eyes, her paws, her meows, and I understand her. I really love you, Cici.
Ciao!
Zlata

Friday, August 14, 1992

Dear Mimmy,

Last night the Bobars came to listen to RFI, the way they do every night. Bojana and I were playing cards. We were all relaxed somehow and forgot for a moment that we are living in a war. The shelling started at around 9:30. Out of the blue, the way it usually does. We raced over to Nedo's place. The shooting died down around midnight and we returned home. You can't relax for even a second!

Zlata

Sunday, August 16, 1992

Dear Mimmy,

Daddy has a hernia. He's lost a lot of weight and carrying the water was too much for him. The doctor has told him that he mustn't lift anything heavy anymore. Mustn't? But somebody has to bring the water! Mommy will have to do it alone now. How will she manage?

Zlata

Tuesday, August 18, 1992

Dear Mimmy,

Mommy is carrying home the water. It's hard on

her, but she has to do it. The water hasn't come back on. Nor has the electricity.

I didn't tell you, Mimmy, but I've forgotten what it's like to have water pouring out of a tap, what it's like to shower. We use a jug now. The jug has replaced the shower. We wash dishes and clothes like in the Middle Ages. This war is taking us back to olden times. And we take it, we suffer it, but we don't know for how long?

Zlata

Friday, August 21, 1992

Dear Mimmy,

I'm not in any of the classes I thought I'd be in at summer school. I've signed up for the literature and drama club. They gave me Abdulah Sidran's "Sarajevo Prayer" to recite. It's great.

Zlata

Tuesday, August 25, 1992

Dear Mimmy,

I go regularly to summer school. I like it. We're together. We don't think about the shelling or the war. Maja and Lela, who help our teacher Irena Vidovic, cheer us up. We write, we recite, we spend

the hours together. It takes me back to the days before the war. I'm also glad to be able to go out into the street. True, it's not far away (200 meters from my house), but I've finally stepped outside. Daddy takes me. Children mustn't walk in the street alone in Sarajevo. I was already going stir crazy. And I "do" myself up, I wear something nice. I mustn't show off too much?
Ciao!
Zlata

Saturday, August 29, 1992

Dear Mimmy,

I'm feeling good today. There's no shooting, I go to summer school, play with Maja, Bojana and Nedo. We fool around, we have our own kind of humor. Sometimes we laugh so much we even forget about the war. We simply get carried away and it's peacetime again. But only until something bursts or explodes. Then we come back to reality. Sometimes I think that if it weren't for them I don't know how I'd be able to stand it. Thank you Maja, Bojana and Nedo, for making it easier for me to take everything that's happening, for killing my boredom and my thoughts about all these ugly things.

Remember them, Mimmy, don't ever forget them. I certainly won't.

Your Zlata

Thursday, September 3, 1992

Dear Mimmy,

The days are passing by more pleasantly. There's no shooting in our neighborhood, but we've been without electricity now for more than a month. If only the electricity would come back on. If only I could cross the bridge and at least go to Grandma and Granddad's! I'm working on it. I'm putting pressure on Mommy and Daddy. Will it work???? We'll find out!

Zlata

Tuesday, September 8, 1992

Dear Mimmy,

YES! YES! YES! THE ELECTRICITY IS BACK!!!!!!

Tomorrow is Mommy's birthday. I made a paper heart and wrote HAPPY BIRTHDAY on it . . . and I cut a bouquet of roses out of the newspaper.

Mommy started making a cake, the kind you

don't need to cook, and when everything was finished, the electricity came back on . . .
OOOHHHH!!!!!!!
Your Zlata

Dear Mimmy,
Today is Auntie Boda's birthday. We gave her a pair of stockings and a packet of coffee. The *hurmasice* [sweet cakes] were super!
Ciao!
Zlata

Dear Mimmy,
Remember, Mimmy, how I told you about two-and-a-half-year-old little Nejra, whom Samra and Emina keep talking about (how cute and talkative she is), and how I'd like to meet her? Well, she came to the neighborhood today. A shell fell into their apartment and they had to leave the place. Now they're with Samra and Emina. Samra and Emina were right. SHE'S SOOO CUTE!

Samra found a job. She's a mechanical engineer

Zlata writes at her desk even as the sound of machine guns echoes from the hills.

Zlata carries water back to the house, and her father also helps her as they walk through the dangerous streets.

and she's working twelve hours a day now. I hardly ever see her.

Your Zlata

Monday, September 14, 1992

Dear Mimmy,

Today is Alma and Dado's wedding anniversary. We gave them a tie-and-belt holder. We had a good time and a good cake!

Zlata

Tuesday, September 15, 1992

Dear Mimmy,

I have another sad piece of news for you. A boy from my drama club got KILLED! . . . A shell fell in front of the community center and a horrible piece of shrapnel killed him. His name was Eldin and he was a refugee from Grbavica.

Another innocent victim of this disgusting war, another child among the thousands of other children killed in Sarajevo. I feel so sorry, he was a sweet, good boy. Oh, God, what is happening here? Hasn't there been enough!?

Zlata

Thursday, September 17, 1992

Dear Mimmy,

Today is Alma's birthday. We gave her two herbal shampoos. We had a super time, but . . . I looked out the window and saw a flash. I thought it was somebody signaling, that's not unusual in war time. But . . . BOOM!! Shattered glass, falling plaster. A shell fell in front of the shop next door and I saw it all from the fourth floor. We rushed over to Nedo's apartment and watched TV.

The birthday party wasn't bad, but it would have been even better if that shell hadn't spoiled it.

Your Zlata

Friday, September 18, 1992

Dear Mimmy,

That's how we celebrate birthdays here and try to forget the war. We try to brighten up this life of ours, a life that's getting harder and harder by the day. Sometimes I say—this isn't life, it's an imitation of life.

The electricity went off again today. BOO-HOO!!! SNIFFLE-SNIFFLE! MORE DARKNESS! WHAT NOW???

Zlata

Saturday, September 19, 1992

Dear Mimmy,

The electricity came back on last night. YESS!

But . . . it went off again this morning. SNIFFLE!
I HOPE IT COMES ON AGAIN TONIGHT! We
have no problem with water. (KNOCK! KNOCK!—
that's me, knocking on wood for good luck.)

YESSS! The electricity is back on! I'm going to
watch *What Others Say About Us* on TV. YESSS!
Your Zlata

Sunday, September 20, 1992

Dear Mimmy,

YIPPEE! I crossed the bridge today. Finally I got to
go out too! I can hardly believe it. The bridge
hasn't changed. But it's sad, sad because of the post
office, which looks even sadder. It's in the same
place, but it's not the same old post office. The fire
has left its mark. It stands there like a witness to brutal destruction.

The streets aren't the same, not many people
are out, they're worried, sad, everybody rushing
around with bowed heads. All the shop windows
have been broken and looted. My school was hit by
a shell and its top floor destroyed. The theater was

also hit by some disgusting shells, and it's wounded. An awful lot of wonderful old Sarajevo buildings have been wounded.

I went to see Grandma and Granddad. Oh, how we hugged and kissed! They cried with joy. They've lost weight and aged since I last saw them four months ago. They told me I had grown, that I was now a big girl. That's nature at work. Children grow, the elderly age. That's how it is with those of us who are still alive.

And there are lots and lots of people and children in Sarajevo who are no longer among the living. The war has claimed them. And all of them were innocent. Innocent victims of this disgusting war.

We ran into Marijana's mother. They didn't leave. They're alive and well. She told me that Ivana had gone to Zagreb—with a Jewish convoy.

We also went to see our friend Doda. She, too, was surprised when she saw me. She cried. She says I've grown. Slobo (her husband) was wounded, but he's all right now. There's no news of Dejan (her son). It makes her sad.

Dear Mimmy, I have something to confess to you. I dressed up. I put on that nice plaid outfit. My shoes were a bit tight, because my feet have grown, but I survived.

So, that was my encounter with the bridge, the post office, Grandma, Granddad, and with a wounded Sarajevo. If only the war would stop, the wounds would heal!

Ciao!

Zlata

Monday, September 21, 1992

Dear Mimmy,

Yesterday's outing into the streets of Sarajevo made me happy, but sad too. I keep seeing the school, the post office, the nearly empty streets, the worried passers-by, the looted shops.

I boasted to Bojana, Maja and Neda how now I had also seen our school, because until yesterday they had been allowed out but I hadn't. My parents were afraid for me. Still, Maja and Bojana are older than I am.

But now I can say like the others that I'm brave. I walked bravely through the streets of Sarajevo.

They said on the radio yesterday that the last long-distance power line that supplied the city with electricity had been destroyed. That means no electricity tonight. Darkness again.

Your Zlata

Monday, September 28, 1992

Dear Mimmy,

OOOOHHHH! No electricity, no water! The water didn't come on this morning. The "fine gentle-men" turned "Bačcevo" off. OOOHHH!

It was Lela's birthday seven days ago (she's a friend of Maja's). I had my hair cut that day. You know who my hairdresser was? My neighbor Alma, because not a single hairdresser's is open yet. And hair grows!

Two days ago it was Avdo's birthday (Lela's father), but there was shooting that day so we couldn't go. I'm sorry about that because birthdays are the only days when the neighbors relax, spend some time together and cheer up a bit. It's nicer than having us all in the cellar. That's why I look forward to birthdays so much.

Neda came today. It looks like she's really going to Zagreb. There's a Jewish convoy leaving at the beginning of October and she's trying to get on it. God, even Neda is leaving us. Mommy is very sad. Zlata

Wednesday, September 30, 1992

Dear Mimmy,

There's no electricity, and probably won't be any

for a long time. The batteries ran out so Daddy brought in the battery from the car and hooked it up to the radio. Now we can listen to the news. Not music, because we have to save on the battery.

They just said on the radio that lots of Croats and Muslims have been expelled from Grbavica. We're expecting Mommy's relatives, Nedo's parents and Lalo (our friend).

Your Zlata

Thursday, October 1, 1992

Dear Mimmy,

Spring has been and gone, summer has been and gone, and now it's autumn. October has started. And the war is still on. The days are getting shorter and colder. Soon we'll move the stove upstairs to the apartment. But how will we keep warm? God, is anyone thinking of us here in Sarajevo? Are we going to start winter without electricity, water or gas, and with a war going on?

The "kids" are negotiating. Will they finally negotiate something? Are they thinking about us when they negotiate, or are they just trying to outwit each other, and leave us to our fate?

Daddy has been checking the attic and cellar for wood. It looks to me as though part of the furniture is going to wind up in the stove if this keeps up until winter. It seems that nobody is thinking of us, that this madness is going to go on and on. We have no choice, we have to rely on ourselves, to take care of ourselves and find a way to fight off the oncoming winter.

Mommy came home from work in a state of shock today. Two of her colleagues came from Grbavica. It really is true that people are being expelled from there. There's no sign of Mommy's and Nedo's relatives or of Lalo. Nedo is going berserk. Your Zlata

Sunday, October 4, 1992

Dear Mimmy,
YESSS! It's not water!
  YESSS! It's not electricity!
  YESSS! YESSS! YESSS!
  Mirna came to see me!
  My bestest friend.
  MIRNA
Her hair has grown long. She's become a real fashion designer. She has a Dalmatian dog in the neighborhood named Gule. She hasn't lost weight. She's even put some on. After we kissed, we didn't know where to start. We hadn't seen each other for

such a long time. Since it was war that had separated us, that's mostly what we talked about. But the important thing is that we were together. I promised to come and see her this week (if there's no shooting, of course).

Love you, Dear Mimmy,
Zlata

Monday, October 5, 1992

Dear Mimmy,
Grandma and Granddad had gas heating. Grandma cooked at Neda's, because she has a gas stove. Well! No electricity, no water, and, wouldn't you know it, no gas!
Your Zlata

Wednesday, October 7, 1992

Dear Mimmy,
Neda has left after all. We're all sad about it. Mommy more than anybody. We'll miss her, but we have to accept that this war is separating us from our friends. How many more people will leave? I'm sorry, Mimmy, I feel sad, I can't write anymore.
Love,
Zlata

Sunday, October 11, 1992

Dear Mimmy,

Today is a day to be remembered in my family. Today we brought the wood-burning stove into the kitchen. It's nice and warm. Mommy and Daddy and I all had a bath. It was rain water, but it doesn't matter. We're clean, and we didn't freeze, like the past few days.

There's still no electricity or water.

Your Zlata

Wednesday, October 14, 1992

Dear Mimmy,

I'm writing to you again by the light of one of my favorite candles. I lit it with a heavy heart. But we have to get light from somewhere. I went to Mirna's today. She showed me her fashion designs and her dog Gule. He's cute, but he hasn't got any spots on his head.

It was a wonderful two hours. Good news:

THE GAS IS BACK ON!

YESSS!

Zlata

Friday, October 16, 1992

Dear Mimmy,

I sometimes go into the "dangerous room" now,

where the piano is, and the notes keep me company. They take me back to the days before the war. Pictures flash through my mind of Jahorina, the sea, Crnotina, my friends. It makes me sad, it even makes me cry. God, they've taken everything away from me.

Mirna came today. YESSS!

There's still no water or electricity. But, luckily, the gas came back on so it's warm at Grandma and Granddad's.

Your Zlata

Wednesday, October 21, 1992

Dear Mimmy,

Today is Daddy's birthday. I gave him a kiss and a "Happy Birthday, Daddy." We made little sweets *"à la Mirna."*

And now let me explain something to you Mimmy: as you know, I confide in you every day (almost). Well, you know the summer school in our community center? We had a wonderful time together there, did some acting, some reciting, and best of all, some writing too. It was all so nice, until that horrible shell killed our friend Eldin.

Maja is still working with our teacher Irena

Vidovic. And the other day, Maja asks me: "Do you keep a diary, Fipa (my nickname)?"

I say: "Yes."

And Maja says: "Is it full of your own secrets or is it about the war?"

And I say: "Now, it's about the war."

And she says: "Fipa, you're terrific."

She said that because they want to publish a child's diary and it just might be mine, which means—YOU, MIMMY. And so I copied part of you into another notebook and you, Mimmy, went to the City Assembly to be looked at. And I've just heard, Mimmy, that you're going to be published! You're coming out for the UNICEF week! SUPER!

And now super good news: the electricity is back on. But it's 5:45 now and it's gone off already. Samra says it will come back on. Let's hope so.
Ciao!
Zlata

Saturday, October 24, 1992

Dear Mimmy,

You know Lalo and Alma. They live in Grbavica, in the occupied part of Sarajevo. Lalo worked with a group of other prisoners. One day they were sent to collect the bodies of dead Chetniks and were arrested by one of "our" units. A few days later they let them go. That's how Lalo got to Sarajevo, to his mother's, but he left his family behind in Grbavica. He looked for a way to get Alma and the children out of Grbavica through some kind of exchange. And, and, and . . . HE DID IT! SUPER!

Your Zlata

Monday, October 26, 1992

Dear Mimmy,

Today we went to see Alma, Anja and Maja (Lalo's family). They're close by now, they live in one of the Zvijezda tower blocks. They're still upset, although everything turned out all right. The important thing is that they're all together now. They're sad because they had to leave everything behind in Grbavica. Anja is little and she keeps asking when they're going home. How can they tell her when she doesn't understand anything? She wants her dolls, her bed. It's really awful!

Zlata

Tuesday, October 27, 1992

Dear Mimmy,

There's talk at the Bobars' that Maja and Bojana

might be going to Austria. Is that possible? Will they go and leave me too? I don't dare think about it. They're not crazy about the idea either. We'll see what happens. There's talk of another Jewish convoy leaving Sarajevo.

Your Zlata

Thursday, October 29, 1992

Dear Mimmy,

Mommy and Auntie Ivanka (from her office) have received grants to specialize in Holland. They have letters of guarantee, and there's even one for me. But Mommy can't decide. If she accepts, she leaves behind Daddy, her parents, her brother. I think it's a hard decision to make. One minute I think—no, I'm against it. But then I remember the war, winter, hunger, my stolen childhood and I feel like going. Then I think of Daddy, Grandma and Granddad, and I don't want to go. It's hard to know what to do. I'm really on edge, Mimmy, I can't write anymore.

Your Zlata

Monday, November 2, 1992

Dear Mimmy,

Mommy thought it over, talked to Daddy, Grandma and Granddad, and to me, and she's decided to go. The reason for her decision is—ME. What's happening in Sarajevo is already too much for me, and the coming winter will make it even harder. All right. But . . . well, I suppose it's better for me to go. I really can't stand it here anymore. I talked to Auntie Ivanka today and she told me that this war is hardest on the children, and that the children should be got out of the city. Daddy will manage, maybe he'll even get to come with us.

Ciao!

Zlata

Friday, November 6, 1992

Dear Mimmy,

Mommy and Auntie Ivanka are trying to get all their papers, because to get out of Sarajevo you need a heap of papers and signatures. It's now certain that Maja and Bojana will be going to Austria. They signed up for the Jewish convoy. Maybe we'll leave on that convoy too.

Zlata

Dear Mimmy,

We were at the Bobars'. Maja and Bojana are packing their suitcases. They leave tomorrow. It was sad. We were all upset and cried.

You should see, Mimmy, what it's like to pack for such a long trip by candlelight. You think you can see enough to pack, but you can't really. I suppose they managed to pack what they need. We're going to see them off tomorrow. The convoy leaves at nine in the morning.

Mommy didn't manage to get all the necessary papers, so we're staying. We'll take some other convoy.

Zlata

Sunday, November 15, 1992

Dear Mimmy,

An awful lot of people have left Sarajevo. All of them well known. Mommy said: "Sarajevo is leaving." Mommy and Daddy know a lot of them. They talked to them and when they said goodbye, everyone kept saying: "We'll see one another again somewhere, sometime." It was sad. Sad and upsetting. November 14, 1992, is a day Sarajevo will remember. It reminded me of the movies I saw about the Jews in the Second World War.

When we got home, the electricity was back on. Daddy went straight to the cellar to cut some wood with the electric saw. Suddenly he came running back from the cellar, his hands covered in blood. The bleeding was terrible. Mommy immediately took him to the clinic, but they were sent on to the hospital where they sewed up his hand, gave him an anti-tetanus shot and told him to come back for a check-up every three days. He was lucky. He could have lost a finger. He says his mind wasn't on his work, he was thinking about the Jewish municipal center, the departure point for leaving Sarajevo. Well-known people are leaving. Sarajevo will be the poorer for losing so many wonderful people, who made it what it was. It's the war that's making them go, this idiocy that we've been living through for a full seven-and-half months.

A TERRIBLY HARD DAY!

Love,
Zlata

Tuesday, November 17, 1992

Dear Mimmy,

As you can see, I'm left without Maja and Bojana. I

miss them very, very much. Luckily, Nedo is still here. He consoles me and tries to make up for the two of them. And there's Cici. Only, she's sad too, as though she knows that Maja and Bojana have gone. She, in her way, makes these ugly days less ugly.

Zlata

Thursday, November 19, 1992

Dear Mimmy,

Nothing new on the political front. They are adopting some resolutions, the "kids" are negotiating, and we are dying, freezing, starving, crying, parting with our friends, leaving our loved ones.

I keep wanting to explain these stupid politics to myself, because it seems to me that politics caused this war, making it our everyday reality. War has crossed out the day and replaced it with horror, and now horrors are unfolding instead of days. It looks to me as though these politics mean Serbs, Croats and Muslims. But they are all people. They are all the same. They all look like people, there's no difference. They all have arms, legs and heads, they walk and talk, but now there's "something" that wants to make them different.

Among my girlfriends, among our friends, in our

family, there are Serbs and Croats and Muslims. It's a mixed group and I never knew who was a Serb, a Croat or a Muslim. Now politics has started meddling around. It has put an "S" on Serbs, an "M" on Muslims and a "C" on Croats, it wants to separate them. And to do so it has chosen the worst, blackest pencil of all—the pencil of war which spells only misery and death.

Why is politics making us unhappy, separating us, when we ourselves know who is good and who isn't? We mix with the good, not with the bad. And among the good there are Serbs and Croats and Muslims, just as there are among the bad. I simply don't understand it. Of course, I'm "young," and politics are conducted by "grown-ups." But I think we "young" would do it better. We certainly wouldn't have chosen war.

The "kids" really are playing, which is why us kids are not playing, we are living in fear, we are suffering, we are not enjoying the sun and flowers, we are not enjoying our childhood. WE ARE CRYING.

A bit of philosophizing on my part, but I was alone and felt I could write this to you, Mimmy. You understand me. Fortunately, I've got you to talk to. And now,
Love,
Zlata

Friday, November 20, 1992

Dear Mimmy,

Doda has left too, with a Slovenian convoy. We didn't manage to get on it. I was at Mirna's today. Her mother is trying to get them on a convoy too. She'll be going with her mother to Slovenia or Krk [an island off the Croatian coast]. Mommy ran into Marijana's mother—they're going to Zaostrog [a town on the Croatian coast]. Basically, we're all waiting for convoys.

Mirna is coming over on Monday (if there's no shooting, of course). We arranged that Mondays she would come to me and Fridays I would go to her. The condition? That there is no shooting.

STOP SHOOTING!!!

Your Zlata

Wednesday, November 25, 1992

Dear Mimmy,

The shooting really has died down. I can hear the whine of the electric saws. The winter and the power saws have condemned the old trees, shaded walks and parks that made Sarajevo so pretty.

I was sad today. I couldn't bear the thought of the trees disappearing from my park. They've been condemned. God, all the things my park has had to go through! The children have left it, Nina forever, and now the linden, birch, and plane trees are leaving it forever, too. Sad. I couldn't watch, and I can't write any more.

Zlata

Sunday, November 29, 1992

Dear Mimmy,

It's cold. We don't have enough wood, so we're saving on it. There is wood at the market, but, like everything else, only for Deutsche Marks and that's very expensive. I keep thinking that my park's linden, birch and plane trees are probably there with the other wood. They're selling for foreign money now.

Braco Lajtner comes by every day. We have lunch together and since he's alone, he stays until dark. Then he goes home. He goes back to a cold, empty house. That isn't easy either!

Mommy brings home the water and when it rains, we collect the rain water, too, it comes in handy. The days are getting shorter and shorter. Mommy, Daddy and I play cards by candlelight, or we read and talk, and around nine o'clock in the evening Boda, Žika and Nedo come to listen to RFI, and that's how the day ends. It's the same almost every day.

Ciao!

Zlata

Thursday, December 3, 1992

Dear Mimmy,

Today is my birthday. My first wartime birthday. Twelve years old. Congratulations. Happy birthday to me!

The day started off with kisses and congratulations. First Mommy and Daddy, then everyone else. Mommy and Daddy gave me three Chinese vanity cases—with flowers on them!

As usual there was no electricity. Auntie Melica came with her family (Kenan, Naida, Nihad) and gave me a book. And Braco Lajtner came, of course. The whole neighborhood got together in the evening. I got chocolate, vitamins, a heart-shaped soap (small, orange), a key chain with a picture of Maja and Bojana, a pendant made of a stone from Cyprus, a ring (silver) and earrings (bingo!).

The table was nicely laid, with little rolls, fish and rice salad, cream cheese (with Feta), canned corned beef, a pie, and, of course—a birthday cake.

Not how it used to be, but there's a war on. Luckily there was no shooting, so we could celebrate.

It was nice, but something was missing. It's called peace!
Your Zlata

Friday, December 4, 1992

Dear Mimmy,
It's awful in Otes. The place is in flames. We can hear the thunder of the shelling, which is constant, even here, and we're ten kilometers away. Lots of civilians have been killed. We're worried about Braco, Keka, Mikica and Dačo. Mommy keeps listening to the radio. Braco called from the press center last night. What's going to happen to them? Until now, everything down there was fine. There was no shooting, they had food, as if there was no war. You never know where or when this war is going to flare up.
Zlata

Sunday, December 6, 1992

Dear Mimmy,
Sad, sad news. The whole of Otes has been de-

stroyed and burned down. Everything went up in flames. People were killed, they fled and were killed as they ran, they were trapped in the ruins and nobody could help them. Parents were left without their children, children without their parents. Horrible. More horror.

Luckily, Braco, Keka, Mikica and Dačo managed to get out in one piece. Keka, Mikica and Dačo drove out and Braco fled on foot. He ran with his injured leg, falling and hiding, he swam across the Dobrinja river and managed to make it to the radio and television center.

He fled with Mišo Kučer (his best friend, they reported from Otes together). At one point, Mišo was hit, he fell and that was the end of him. Braco barely managed to drag him to a house and then went on running, to save his own life. It's terrible. Terrible when you're powerless to help a friend. Oh, God, dear God, what is happening to us? How much longer?

Your Zlata

Thursday, December 10, 1992

Dear Mimmy,

And so Braco and his family joined the list of hundreds of families in Sarajevo who are left with nothing. Absolutely nothing. Everything they had has been destroyed. But they managed to save their lives. That's the most important thing.

They're at Keka's mother's now. They came to see us. They were sad, they cried. It's awful what they've been through. They need peace and quiet. But where are they going to find that here? We'll help them as much as we can. Mommy has given them a lot of clothes, because it's cold and they have nothing. Other people have helped them too. And will help them again. It's lucky that there are good people around who will give a helping hand to those in need.

Braco is the saddest of all. He cried when he told us about Mišo. TERRIBLE!

Love,

Zlata

Tuesday, December 15, 1992

Dear Mimmy,

I spend all my time with Mikica and Dačo these days. I try to help them forget all the awful things that have happened to them. But they can't forget. It's constantly on their minds. They remember the terrible shelling, the destruction, the flames, and everything they left behind and lost in the flames. Their toys, books, photos, their memories. Dačo is

sorriest about his Alf dolls, and Mikica says: "When I see something or talk about something I think to myself: Oh, I've got that. And then the truth hits me—I don't really have anything anymore." It's really hard. But, we're all helpless. The war has got a hold of us and won't let us go.
Zlata

Dear Mimmy,
Mommy ran into my piano teacher today—Biljana Čanković. She complained to Mommy how she had to hold her piano lessons in the school, and she had no pupils. How can you give lessons when you have no pupils?

Lots of children have left Sarajevo, and for those who are still here it's dangerous to move around the city. The shelling can start out of the blue. She might even lose her job because she has no pupils. It's silly. God, how stupid it is!

Mommy said she'd go to the school headmaster on Monday and arrange something.

And now super news. Mirna can come and sleep over.
Love,
Zlata

Wednesday, December 23, 1992

Dear Mimmy,

NEWS! I'm going to music school. Actually, my piano teacher will be coming here. Since it's too dangerous for children to move around in town. Mirna has signed up too. We have our first lesson on Monday. I've got butterflies in my stomach. See you. Ciao!

Your Zlata

Friday, December 25, 1992

Dear Mimmy,

Today is Christmas. Christmas in wartime. Still, people have tried to make it something special for the children.

Auntie Radmila got me into the group of Caritas children, and so, thanks to her, I got to go to the UNPROFOR [United Nations Protection Force]—PTT [post office] Christmas show. And most interesting of all I got to ride in a real personnel carrier.

As we drove through town I saw Vodoprivreda where Mommy worked (there's nothing left—it's burned down), the Elektroprivreda building (it looks terrible—it's all wounded), the UNIS building (all burned down), the old tobacco plant (an ash heap), and the *Oslobodjenje* newspaper building (it looks awful). I saw but I couldn't believe my eyes. Sarajevo really has been wounded, not to say destroyed.

Tifa, Goga Magaš, five girls and a boy were in the show. They did some silly dance and then had a smoke, and there was that singer Alma, the one who always goes: "Aooooa . . ."

Then they gave out the Christmas presents and sweets. The children started pushing, almost fighting over them. I wasn't one of the lucky ones to get anything, because I didn't elbow my way through. What can I say? A nice little girl from a nice family. The "little lady" didn't get her present. Then the French soldiers began to sing. They were wonderful. We went there at noon and left at five o'clock in the afternoon. Since it was too late to go home, I spent the night at Grandma's and Granddad's.

I'm there now. It's warm. I told them all about what I saw. Grandma made me pancakes. For my sweet tooth!

Ciao.

Zlata

Saturday, December 26, 1992

Dear Mimmy,

Went to Auntie Radmila's for Christmas today. She

made all sorts of things. She gave us a wonderful treat and I even got a little Christmas present. Afterward we went to Braco Lajtner's but he wasn't home, just Auntie Vilma and Auntie Micika. Auntie Vilma is Braco's aunt. He brought her to stay with him because of the cold. Auntie Micika is his neighbor. She was his mother's best friend. She has no heat and Braco felt sorry for her so he brought her to live with him. You know how old she is? Eighty-seven. And full of life.

Zlata

Monday, December 28, 1992

Dear Mimmy,

I've been walking my feet off these past few days.

I'm at home today. I had my first piano lesson. My teacher and I kissed and hugged, we hadn't seen each other since March. Then we moved on to Czerny, Bach, Mozart and Chopin, to the étude, the invention, the sonata and the "piece." It's not going to be easy. But I'm not going to school now and I'll give it my all. It makes me happy. Mimmy, I'm now in my fifth year of music school.

You know, Mimmy, we've had no water or electricity for ages. When I go out and when there's no shooting it's as if the war were over, but this business with the electricity and water, this darkness, this winter, the shortage of wood and food, brings me back to earth and then I realize that the war is still on. Why? Why on earth don't those "kids" come to some agreement? They really are playing games. And it's us they're playing with.

As I sit writing to you, my dear Mimmy, I look over at Mommy and Daddy. They are reading. They lift their eyes from the page and think about something. What are they thinking about? About the book they are reading or are they trying to put together the scattered pieces of this war puzzle? I think it must be the latter. Somehow they look even sadder to me in the light of the oil lamp (we have no more wax candles, so we make our own oil lamps). I look at Daddy. He really has lost a lot of weight. The scales say twenty-five kilos, but looking at him I think it must be more. I think even his glasses are too big for him. Mommy has lost weight too. She's shrunk somehow, the war has given her wrinkles. God, what is this war doing to my parents? They don't look like my old Mommy and Daddy anymore. Will this ever stop? Will our suffering stop so that my parents can be what they used to be— cheerful, smiling, nice-looking?

This stupid war is destroying my childhood, it's

destroying my parents' lives. WHY? STOP THE WAR! PEACE! I NEED PEACE!

I'm going to play a game of cards with them!
Love from your Zlata

Wednesday, December 30, 1992

Dear Mimmy,
Tomorrow night people will be seeing out the old year and ringing in the new all over the world. I remember previous New Year's Eves, I wonder what they are like in the normal world. And here???? In Sarajevo???

In Sarajevo we're ringing in the New Year so that we can forget the old as quickly as possible, in the hope that the New Year will bring us peace. That's all we want. When there is peace, then it's a good and happy year. That is what we the (innocent) people of Sarajevo wish. And just because we are innocent, our wish should be answered. We don't deserve to suffer like this anymore.
Zlata

Friday, January 1, 1993

Dear Mimmy,
HAPPY NEW YEAR!!!

May this year bring us peace, happiness, love, re-united families and friends.

Now let me tell you how we saw out the old year and rang in the new.

Yesterday we (Mommy, Daddy and I) first went to Melica's for her birthday. We had lunch there. Melica gave us a jar of pickled carrots as her New Year's present.

We came home. Mommy went to fetch the water, and Daddy and I stayed in the house. When Mommy got back we sat around for a while, made sandwiches with margarine (the package of winter food supplies Mommy got at the office included margarine), cream cheese and liver sausage. "Fantastic" sandwiches! Yum-Yum!

Around eight o'clock we started getting drowsy. Then Auntie Boda burst in, got us onto our feet and we all went to their place, where we had "turkey" (a can of beef) and real Emmenthal cheese. Around ten o'clock we all started getting drowsy again, and then somebody remembered to turn on the radio. And on the radio were the Nadrealisti [Surrealists, a Sarajevo comedy group]. We all woke up. And so, bit by bit, the New Year came round. Žika opened a bottle of champagne (he had been saving it for the end of the war, but since the end

Zlata, who loves books, reads by candlelight.

isn't in sight he opened it now), and we all kissed (Grandma, Žika, Boda, Mommy, Daddy, Cici and I). Nedo was missing, but he had gone off with his friends. Mommy and Daddy gave me a comb and barrette, the Bobars gave me a musical egg (it has a light sensor) and Slime. They gave Mommy some nail-polish remover, and we gave them some potatoes, onions and sour cabbage. Oh, wow!

And that's how we spent the evening until 1:30 in the morning. We were dead tired when we got home. It was 2:00 A.M. before we got to bed. We slept like babies.

Once again, Mimmy, Happy New Year to you and all the people of Sarajevo.
Love,
Zlata

Tuesday, January 5, 1993

Dear Mimmy,
Today we received a package from Neda in Zagreb. It came through the Adventist Church. It was full of all sorts of things. It made us happy, but also sad. I liked the tangerines, chocolate bars and "Nutella" best.

Auntie Irena, my summer school teacher, is still looking out for us. She brightened up our days at the summer school, while it lasted, and now through UNICEF [United Nations International Children's Fund] she's managed to get us thermal underwear. She brought them over today. The underpants are red, and the top has red and white stripes. Thank you Auntie Irena. Thank you UNICEF.

Ciao,
Zlata

Wednesday, January 6, 1993

Dear Mimmy,

It's freezing. Winter has definitely come to town. I used to love and enjoy it so much, but now it's a very disagreeable guest in Sarajevo.

Our flowers have frozen. They were in the rooms we didn't heat. We live in the kitchen now. That's the only room we heat and we manage to get the temperature up to 63.4°F. Cicko is with us. I'm afraid he might get sick, because birds are sensitive to winter.

We moved the mattresses into the kitchen and now we sleep here. (Don't make me tell you how many sweaters and pullovers we wear over our pajamas.) The kitchen is now our kitchen and our sitting room and our bedroom and even our bathroom. We have an unusual way of bathing. We spread out the sheets of plastic and then—the basin becomes our bathtub, the jug our shower, and so on.

Daddy's got frostbite on his fingers from cutting the wood in the cold cellar. They look awful. His fingers are swollen and now they're putting some cream on them, but they itch badly. Poor Daddy.

Tomorrow I'm probably going to Grandma's and Granddad's. They have gas heating.

Zlata

Friday, January 8, 1993

Dear Mimmy,

In Geneva "all three warring sides" are trying to reach some agreement. I don't think it will amount to anything. I don't believe anyone.

Still no electricity or water.

Tomorrow, Mimmy, I'm going to my old teacher (she's retired now) for a math lesson. Mirna is coming with me. The two of us practiced a little today but we seem to have forgotten everything. We'll see tomorrow.

And tomorrow Mommy and Auntie Ivanka are going to the Holiday Inn to see about the Slovenian convoy. Maybe we'll leave on it.

Now for the main thing. Yesterday Auntie Boda received a letter from Maja and Bojana. YIPPEE, HOORAY! I read it today. Everything is really super. They live in a big house—700 square meters. They go to school, too. They've been eating all sorts of wonderful things—tomatoes, Pi-Pi orangeade, Camembert . . . YUMMY-YUMMY! Their thoughts are with us and they are sad for us.

Zlata

Saturday, January 9, 1993

Dear Mimmy,

They killed Vice-Premier Hakija Turajlić, my work-shop teacher's husband. Everybody says he was a wonderful man. What a shame.

My math lesson at my teacher's was a success. We learned three new lessons. The arithmetic mean, ratios and percentages.

No electricity, no water.

Zlata

Monday, January 11, 1993

Dear Mimmy,

It's snowing. A real winter's day. The snowflakes are huge. If only I could go out sledding, since I can't go to Jahorina. But, there's a war on, Zlata! The war won't allow it. You have to sit in the house and watch the snowflakes play, and enjoy yourself that way. Or get your enjoyment from remembering the good old days, before the reality of war brings you back to earth.

I watch people lugging water. They are using sleds for that now. We left ours at Jahorina, so we have to borrow Auntie Boda's.

Thank God we didn't have to stay in the cellar for long. The shooting wasn't that bad. Otherwise we would have frozen stiff down there. Are they thinking about us after all????

Zlata

Friday, January 15, 1993

Dear Mimmy,

Just so you know, the war is still on. But I'm sick, Oohhh! Yesterday I had a sore throat but no temperature. Last night I got a cream for my throat and it doesn't hurt anymore, but I have a temperature: 99.5°F or 100.4°F or 101.3°F. A temperature, and I've got math tomorrow! SNIFFLE!!!

Mirna came to see me today. She kept her distance from me.

Zlata

Dear Mimmy,

I'm over my little flu. I went to my math class yesterday. It's going well.

And now listen to this. Electricity has returned to the city, but only for priority consumers, and that's not us. But it is one of our neighbors. He gives us a little through a cable, so we can get some warmth, use the stove to cook something, and watch TV. It's great! And there's water too. How little we Sarajevo people need to make us happy.

Ciao,

Zlata

Dear Mimmy,

I'm getting ready to go to Nejra's birthday party. I'm wearing black tights (thick, of course), a red turtleneck under a white blouse, a kilt and red cardigan sweater. As you can see, I've dressed up.

The party was nice. We gave Nejra a bunny. The old crowd from the neighborhood was there.

Mimmy, I've noticed that I don't write to you anymore about the war or the shooting. That's probably because I've become used to it. All I care about is that the shells don't fall within 50 meters of my

house, that we've got wood, water and, of course, electricity. I can't believe I've become used to all this, but it seems I have. Whether it's being used to it, fighting for survival or something else, I don't know.
Ciao,
Zlata

Monday, February 1, 1993

Dear Mimmy,
It's February. In three days it will have been ten months of hell, blood, horror. Today is Kenan's birthday. We can't go, because they're shooting again. God, I keep thinking this is going to stop, but the war just goes on and on.
Zlata

Friday, February 5, 1993

Dear Mimmy,
Today we celebrated Žika's and Bojana's birthdays. (Today is actually Bojana's birthday. Žika's was on February 2.) I just wonder how Bojana celebrated it in Austria. Probably not like us, with an oil lamp, beef and Feta cheese sandwiches, rolls, tea, marzipan made of flour and wartime *hurmašice* cakes.

It's been a long time since we heard from Maja and Bojana. I hope they're all right. Right now I'm doing my math and practicing on the piano. Mirna can hardly wait to finish the fifth and sixth grade in school so she can move on to the seventh. She thinks she'll feel older. I don't know what I would like??? I just know that the war is stealing years of our life and childhood from us.

Along with Braco Lajtner, we also have Seka (Bokica's sister) here. She has no heating so she stays here with us until dark and then goes home. She spent the night here a few times too.
Zlata

Monday, February 8, 1993

Dear Mimmy,

Bajo and Goga are coming. They're our friends. Their daughter Tia is sixteen. She's in Czechoslovakia. They're alone. They sometimes talk to Tia through ham radios, but they rarely get letters from her. It makes them sad. Letters are something very precious here, they bring joy, even though they also bring tears. Bajo's brother sends them packages from Belgrade and they always bring something over for me; it's a real treat for

Mommy and Daddy when they bring cigarettes and some coffee.

Your Zlata

Friday, February 12, 1993

Dear Mimmy,

Again there's no electricity, not even for priority cases. We're back to the dark and chopping wood again. I was looking forward to spending time with my music, with Mozart, Bach and the others, but now I can't. It's freezing in the piano room. The room has become "dangerous" again??? I really don't feel up to all this.

Mirna was here today. We practiced math a bit and later played with our Barbie dolls.

Zlata

Monday, February 15, 1993

Dear Mimmy,

Yesterday was Haris' birthday party. It wasn't bad. There were lots of people. In fact it would have been perfect if the grown-ups hadn't started talking politics. I'm sick to death of politics. YUCK!

Well, Haris' birthday ends this string of February

birthdays. Never mind. I like them so much because they remind me of peacetime (provided there's no shooting, of course).

Your Zlata

Dear Mimmy,

Something tremendous happened yesterday. We had real live French people in the house. Aha, yes we did, French people.

They asked me some questions and in the end told me they'd be doing a report on me. It's supposed to be filmed at the Viječnica University Library. That will be interesting, to see the library (it's burned down), and a real film camera.

Zlata

Tuesday, February 23, 1993

Dear Mimmy,

Nothing came of the report about me. There's no electricity, no cameraman and it can't be filmed. So I don't get to see the library. I'm really disappointed. But, it can't be helped.

Yesterday Mommy and Daddy arranged with Mirna's parents to see whether we can finish the school year privately. Mirna and I would study together, and our parents would help us with whatever we didn't understand and that way we would make use of all this boring time on our hands. And we'd finish the year. We'll see! First we have to see with the school whether it's possible. The convoy has fallen through. I think we'll have to give up on it. You can't get out of Sarajevo. They won't let you. Who won't? It doesn't even matter . . . We'll stay where we are. This can't go on forever. Perhaps the "kids" will get tired of their game.

Your Zlata

Thursday, February 25, 1993

Dear Mimmy,

We got a letter from Keka and Neda. It made us all sad and we cried again. It's not easy for them either.

Auntie Ivanka received a package from Belgrade and brought me all sorts of things. Chocolate, ham (OOOH!), instant mashed potatoes, sugar, coffee, macaroni. Thank you Auntie Ivanka! And Auntie Radmila brought me powdered milk. Imagine how everyone is thinking of me, a child hungry for everything. I got three letters from French children through a humanitarian organization. They were

colorful New Year's cards that arrived late. They were full of love and warm wishes for peace in Sarajevo. One of them came with colored magic markers, which I used to draw them a heart.
Zlata

Monday, March 1, 1993

Dear Mimmy,

Our idea of finishing fifth grade fell through. It can't be done because they're seriously thinking about reopening the schools. Schools? All the schools near me are either unusable or full of refugees. Where? They're talking about using the Teacher Training College (which is near us). That would be good.

Your Zlata

Friday, March 5, 1993

Dear Mimmy,

There is now gas on our side, too, here on the left bank of the Miljacka. But how to get it? Our neighbor Enver helped us out. He let us hook up to his gas supply. Žika, Avdo and Daddy were "gas men" today. They put a heater in our stove and now it's warm. Daddy doesn't have to chop wood (that is, furniture) anymore. We attached the gas stove to it too, so now we can cook on gas. SUPER! How much nicer everything is, how much easier we breathe. Now we can sleep in the corner of the sitting room again and the apartment looks nicer.

Zlata

Wednesday, March 10, 1993

Dear Mimmy,

There's a terrible problem. We've run out of bird food for Cicko. There's no bird food anywhere in town. What can we do?

We cook him rice, but he won't touch it. Auntie Ivanka brought unglazed rice, and he nibbled at it. He won't touch cooked peas. The only thing he seems willing to try is bread crumbs. We raised the alarm. We want to save our Cicko—we can't let him starve.

Today Mommy got bird food from Auntie Radmila and a colleague at work. They took it from the beaks of their own pets. Oh, you should see, Mimmy, how Cicko eats! But we mustn't give him too much, we have to save. We only have enough for a few days.

And this evening, this evening when Žika came to listen to RFI, he brought a bag of the precious grain for our Cicko. How lucky you are Cicko. See how people are thinking of you? Now he has a decent amount of food. He won't die of hunger.

There, even birds are sharing their food, helping each other out, like people. I'm so happy. Enjoy yourself, Cicko!

Zlata

Monday, March 15, 1993

Dear Mimmy,

I'm sick again. My throat hurts, I'm sneezing and coughing. And spring is around the corner. The second spring of the war. I know from the calendar, but I don't see it. I can't see it because I can't feel it. All I can see are the poor people still lugging water, and the even poorer invalids—young people without arms and legs. They're the ones who had the fortune or perhaps the misfortune to survive.

There are no trees to blossom and no birds, because the war has destroyed them as well. There is no sound of birds twittering in springtime. There aren't even any pigeons—the symbol of Sarajevo. No noisy children, no games. Even the children no longer seem like children. They've had their childhood taken away from them, and without that they can't be children. It's as if Sarajevo is slowly dying, disappearing. Life is disappearing. So how can I feel spring, when spring is something that awakens life, and here there is no life, here everything seems to have died.

I'm sad again, Mimmy. But you have to know that I'm getting sadder and sadder. I'm sad whenever I think, and I have to think.

Your Zlata

Friday, March 19, 1993

Dear Mimmy,

News. Nedo got himself a job with UNPROFOR. He'll be working as a translator for the observers. He came straight to my door last night with his helmet and flak jacket on. I almost fainted. Of course, I immediately tried on the helmet, but the flak jacket—it's so heavy! I almost fell over when I put it on. That's the good news. The rest, the rest is the usual. STUPID!

Ciao!

Zlata

Thursday, March 25, 1993

Dear Mimmy,

Slobo is very sick. He's in the hospital. He hasn't

been well at all ever since Doda left. He's fallen ill from grief. The war has destroyed his life. His Doda is in Slovenia, Dejan and mother in Subotica. He's alone. Now he has illness for company. And it won't let him go. He's getting worse. I don't know anything about illness, except when you have a temperature and a sore throat, but they say he is seriously ill. Mommy and Daddy went to see him in the hospital. They say he doesn't look well or feel well. They mentioned some kind of radiation. I really feel sorry for Slobo!

Your Zlata

Saturday, March 27, 1993

Dear Mimmy,

The days go by, March is almost over and has brought us nothing good. It's as though we were stuck in the mud and there's nobody to offer a helping hand and pull us out. And we just keep waiting, stuck like that. If only the convoys had moved out. Wherever I would have gone, it would have been better than this. To tell you the truth, Mimmy, I don't understand why they won't let people leave. Why, this way we're all going to either die or go crazy.

Still, there are some nice things happening to

Dnevnik rada

ručali i večerali suho, jer je nestalo plina, jučer. Kao što znaš nemamo ni struje i tako da smo svi na pragu samoubistva. KATASTROFA? Joj, Mimmy, ne mogu više. Muka mi je od svega. Strašno sam umorna od svih ovih ?SSS.? Izvini, psujem, ali zaista ne mogu više, dosta je, zaista. Sve je veća mogućnost da se ubijem. Ako me svi ovi kretenu i odozgo i odozdo, ne ubiju prije. Strašno sam popustila. HOĆU DA VRISTIM DA LUPAM, DA UBIJAM. Pa, i ja sam ljudsko biće i ja imam svoje granice. JOOOJ!

Muka mi je!

OVO ŠTO JE
DOLE NAPISANO
NAPISANO JE U
BOLJEM RASPOLOŽENJU
Rasplakaću se!

Voli te Tibaš

AAAAA —ISCURI

——————>

Zlata with her mother and father. "What is this war doing to my parents? They don't look like my Mommy and Daddy anymore."

me. Today I had visitors. Two French journalists. They're young and great. The most terrific thing of all is that I talked to them in English the whole time.

They really made my day. It started off like any other, with me bored and thinking about how long things are going to go on like this, but it ended nicely.

Zlata

Monday, April 5, 1993

Dear Mimmy,

On March 31, 1993, I started school. They've already divided us into Grade VI-I and Grade VI-2. I'm in VI-2. Anesa, Nežla, Nerma and some other girls, whom I don't know, are in my class. It's not what it used to be, but it doesn't matter. The important thing is to go to school, then it won't be so boring. We have all our regular subjects except for physical education and workshop.

Our class-mistress is Zlata Grabovac. And, she's SUPER. Our math teacher—he likes to joke around but I don't understand his lectures very well and so my class-mistress explains them to me. Enisa (our language teacher)—not bad, young, actually, quite good. Azra—the goddess of biology. Branislava (history and geography)—lectures slowly and calmly, and is dreadfully strict during exams. Marija (physics)—no comment. OK. Vlasta (English)—as I said, super. Our art teacher thinks we're all Picasso or Rembrandt or Van Gogh. Slavica (music)—nothing new (she hasn't lost weight, but the dye in her hair has faded and she's gone gray).

There, Mimmy, now you even know my teachers.
Your Zlata

Thursday, April 8, 1993

Dear Mimmy,

More terrible, sad news today. Our dear, beloved Cicko has died. He just toppled over and that was it. He wasn't sick. It happened suddenly.

He was singing. Now he's not cold anymore. The poor thing got through the winter, we found him food. And he left it all. Maybe he had had enough of this war. It was all too much for him—he had felt cold and hunger and now he has gone forever. I cried, but Mommy was worse than me. We're going to miss him dreadfully. We loved him so much, he was a member of the family. He lived with us for seven years. That's a long time. Daddy buried him in the yard. His cage is empty. No more Cicko.
Your Zlata

Thursday, April 15, 1993

Dear Mimmy,

We've been without Cicko for seven days now. I miss him. He's left a big gap. I keep thinking I'm going to hear his lovely song, but there's no Cicko, and no song. But life goes on.

I already have an A in language, an A in biology, two As in English, two As in art, and it looks as though I'm going to get a B on my history test.

As for food, Coke, sweets and even my favorite drink, Pi-Pi orangeade, come my way often these days. All thanks to my Nedo, who brings them to me from UNPROFOR.

Zlata

Saturday, April 17, 1993

Dear Mimmy,

Seka is beside herself. It looks as though she's going to be evicted from Bokica's apartment. There are lots of refugees here, Mimmy, lots of people made "homeless" by the war. The war expelled them, destroyed and set fire to their apartments. They have to have a roof over their heads somewhere. And there are not many roofs to be had. There are empty apartments, belonging to people who have left Sarajevo, and they could give the "homeless" a roof over their heads but things seem to be getting complicated. Some people are being moved in, and others moved out. They're replacing one tragedy with another. How awful all this is. Sometimes I don't understand a thing. Actually, I don't understand this war. I know it's stupid, and since it's stupid so is everything else. And I know it won't bring anyone happiness.

The political situation is stupidity in motion. Great BIG stupidity. I really don't know whether to go on living and suffering, to go on hoping, or to take a rope and just . . . be done with it. If things go on like this, I'll be twenty in a few years time. If it turns out to be another "Lebanon," as they keep saying, I'll be thirty. Gone will be my childhood, gone my youth, gone my life. And I'll die and this war still won't be over. And when Mommy says to me: "We'll go away, Zlata," again I feel like killing myself. Sure, all they're waiting for out there is for some Alica, Malik and Zlata to come along . . .
Your Zlata

Monday, April 19, 1993

Dear Mimmy,
I've grown, Mimmy. I have nothing to wear. Everything's too small, too tight, too short for me.

I arranged with Braco to see if I could use some of Martina's things; Keka wrote to me and said to take what I need.

I went there today. I was in Martina and Matea's room. The room was empty, just their photographs, a few of their things, which they must be missing, broken windows, dust. The two of them aren't there. The room is sad and so am I.

After that first encounter with the room, I remembered why I had come. Among Martina's things I found myself a black, patchwork skirt, white tennis shoes, walking shoes and a more feminine pair.

I remembered what Keka had said in her letter: "Take anything that can brighten up your day, Zlata, and enjoy it if you can, because tomorrow will come. You can be sure of it."

What would brighten up my day is peace, what would brighten up my day is to have them back and to have back everything I've lost.

Ciao!

Zlata

Sunday, April 25, 1993

Dear Mimmy,

I have sad news for you again. Bobo is dead. Auntie

Disa's Bobo. He was killed in Melica's garden. It was a sniper. Awful. Everybody was in the garden and the sniper picked him out. What a shame. He was wonderful. He's left behind little Ines, his four-year-old little girl, who is a refugee with her mother.

Auntie Diša is almost out of her mind with grief. She keeps saying: "Maybe he didn't die. It isn't true. My son will come back to me."

Horrible, Mimmy, I can't write to you anymore. Your Zlata

Tuesday, April 27, 1993

Dear Mimmy,

Yesterday we got new neighbors. Haris and Alemka, or Alenka (I don't know whether it's an "m" or an "n"). They got married yesterday. They're in Nedo's apartment. He generously opened the doors of his apartment to them and now they're living with him. Nedo and Haris are good friends from before (they're both refugees from Grbavica). Nedo was the best man at their wedding. Our neighborhood is growing.

Today we got a package from Keka. And, as usual, it had all sorts of things in it. Now our food stocks

have been fortified. The Milka was great! That's real chocolate!
Ciao!
Zlata

Wednesday, April 28, 1993

Dear Mimmy,
We've just come home from Haris and Alenka's. Like the good neighbors that we are, we went to introduce ourselves and to congratulate them. You only get married the first time once. Nedo was there too. We had a nice time, but the "boys" started shelling again. They say shells fell on the Beograd Hotel and on the kindergarten in Dalmatinska Street. Our own tiresome sniper, we call him "Jovo," was in a playful mood today. He's really out of his mind. There he goes! He just fired another bullet, to shake us up.
Ciao!
Zlata

Sunday, May 2, 1993

Dear Mimmy,
Do you remember May 2, 1992, the worst day in this

misery of a life? I often say that maybe it wasn't the most awful day, but it was the first of the most awful days, and so I think of it as the worst. I'll never forget the stench of the cellar, the hunger, the shattering glass, the horrible shelling. We went for twelve hours without food or water, but the worst thing was the fear, huddling in the corner of the cellar, and the uncertainty of what was going to happen. Not understanding what was happening. It gives me the shivers just to think about it.

It's been a year since then, a year in which every day has been May 2. But here I am still alive and healthy, my family is alive and well, sometimes we have electricity, water and gas and we get the odd scrap of food. KEEP GOING. But for how long, does anyone really know?
Zlata

Monday, May 3, 1993

Dear Mimmy,
Auntie Boda and Žika got letters from Bojana and Maja today. They're okay, they eat, drink, worry . . .

Apart from the letters, we leafed through the Bosnian language dictionary. I don't know what to say, Mimmy. Perhaps an excess of the letter "h," which until now was looked on as a spelling mistake.[6] What's to be done????

It's been a long time since I wrote to you about what I've been reading. Well, let me tell you now: *Famous Seafarers, Three Hearts, The Spark of Life, The Jottings of an Ana, Bare Face, The Wrath of the Angels, The Famous Five, A Man, a Woman and a Child, Territorial Rights, Somebody Else's Little Girl, I Was a Drug Addict, Delusion* and ... and I also often leaf through the photographs in cookbooks—it makes me feel as though I've eaten what I'm looking at. Zlata

Tuesday, May 4, 1993

Dear Mimmy,

I've been thinking about politics again. No matter how stupid, ugly and unreasonable I think this division of people into Serbs, Croats and Muslims is, these stupid politics are making it happen. We're all waiting for something, hoping for something, but there's nothing. Even the Vance-Owen peace plan looks as though it's going to fall through. Now

[6] This may be referring to the "h" once given to certain local Turkish and other words and pronunciation, and later dropped from usage.

these maps are being drawn up, separating people, and nobody asks them a thing. Those "kids" really are playing around with us. Ordinary people don't want this division, because it won't make anybody happy—not the Serbs, not the Croats, not the Muslims. But who asks ordinary people? Politics asks only its own people.

Your Zlata

Thursday, May 6, 1993

Dear Mimmy,

Today—drama in the house.

I was sitting in the room, reading, when suddenly something darted across the floor. And you know what it was, Mimmy? A tiny little mouse. So small that I barely recognized it for what it was. He ran under the built-in bookcase in the niche by the wall. Mommy screamed. She climbed onto a chair and then ran off into my room. I know she would have liked to run out of the house, but . . . THERE'S A WAR ON.

What to do? We had to catch it. But how? I ran off to get Cici (cats are mouse specialists), and Daddy and Braco reached for their tools, screwdrivers and things. They took down the bookcase. Cici was waiting in ambush. Daddy and Braco unscrewed the shelves and I took down the books. And Mommy? She was in my room waiting, of course. When they removed the bookcase they found a little hole in the wall where he had escaped. They blocked off the hole with plaster, put everything back and tried to persuade Mommy to come back in and move around the house normally.

We tried to convince her, but she was all in knots. We moved Cici in with us. Now she sleeps in our apartment and Mommy feels a bit safer (I hope). The mouse has run away and probably won't come back. Mommy doesn't believe it, though.

Just when we thought we had resolved the problem of the mouse, he began to scratch at the wall again. He wanted to get back in. He's really silly. Doesn't he realize that we're trying to get rid of him? He's an animal, after all, Mimmy.

Mommy is going out of her mind. I have to do something about that mouse. I'm going to talk to Cici and have her fix things.
Ciao!
Zlata

Saturday, May 8, 1993

Dear Mimmy,
I went to music school today and saw the market-

place. It's got everything. Everything you can think of. People are selling everything.

I wondered where all these things come from and then I remembered my first wartime encounter with the streets of Sarajevo, I remembered the broken display windows and missing goods. Is that the answer? Who's behind it? It doesn't really matter. What was done was bad enough, but it's even worse to be selling all that now, and to be doing so for expensive foreign money . . . You should see all the food! Meanwhile we're going hungry and are grateful for anything we can get. How can you buy anything when one egg costs 5 Deutsche Marks, a bar of chocolate 20 DM, biscuits 40 DM, a package of coffee 120 DM. I could go on and on. Who's it for, if we ordinary people can't afford it? But, never mind . . . I have my Nedo, we get our packages. I have Auntie Radmila, Auntie Ivanka, Gogo and Bajo, Jelica, Auntie Boda, Grandma and Granddad, and sooooo many other good people. I suppose there'll be an end to this kind of market and smuggling. I suppose the shops will open up to ordinary people. Ordinary people, Mimmy, receive humanitarian aid, they help each other out with packages, and now, whenever and wherever they can, they are planting vegetables to survive. Window sills and balconies have been turned into vegetable gardens.

Flowers have been replaced with lettuce, onions, parsley, carrots, beets, tomatoes and all sorts of other things. Instead of those beautiful geraniums we now have lettuce, onions, parsley and carrots. We gave the remaining seeds to Melica to plant, because she has a garden.

Ciao!

Zlata

Friday, May 14, 1993

Dear Mimmy,

Ciao! It's now 9:20 and I'm sitting at the desk in my room. The door is open and the sounds of RFI are coming in from the kitchen. Sitting in the kitchen are Žika, Boda, Nedo, Haris, Alemka (we figured out that it's an "m"), Mommy and Daddy.

Haris and Alemka are here for the first time. They're wonderful. But then again they couldn't be anything but wonderful because they're Nedo's friends. I had dinner at their place last night. I ate three-and-a-half dumplings (Boda's) and four pancakes (Alemka's). I ate too much. I'm going to drink down a jerrycan of water now.

Yesterday, Auntie Boda received a letter from Maja and Bojana. The two of them are great and are having a great time.

And now for an amazing piece of news. Nedo is leaving Sarajevo (temporarily). He's going to either Zagreb or Split. Since he works for UNPROFOR he's entitled to annual leave. Maybe he'll see his girlfriend. He certainly deserves to.

Nothing new on the western, pardon me, on the school front. The As are piling up.

Zlata

Monday, May 17, 1993

Dear Mimmy,

There's never a dull moment in our house. The mouse is up to its usual tricks. He's quiet, disappears for days and then begins to scratch at the wall again. Daddy even got hold of some glue. I'm afraid Mommy is going to go crazy.

Cici doesn't care about the mouse anymore. You know why, Mimmy? She's in love. You don't believe me? Honestly, she's fallen in love. I looked out the window today and watched her with a tomcat on the roof. The tomcat started strutting over to her. They gazed at each other, and then came closer. Then they sniffed each other and looked as if they were kissing. Then he left, and she stood there looking confused, meowing.

Nedo left today. Have a safe journey Nedo, and

come back to us! Daddy doesn't think he will come back. But I want him to come back, and that's why I think he will.

Your Zlata

Dear Mimmy,

I've had a haircut. Short. Mommy gives me funny looks. She says I look unusual to her. But I like it. I wanted to change something. Mimmy, I'm sick of everything, so I made a change, on the top of my head.

In the end, Seka did receive eviction papers after all. Mommy has been going to her place to help her pack Bokica's things. She comes home miserable. She's packing away Bokica's things. Bokica and Srdjan's life together, because those things are really their life. Mommy brought home a photo album and some other things of theirs, the rest they'll store in the cellar. It's like being shelled again. Bokica and Srdjan don't even know about it. They're in Dubrovnik, and there's no mail going in or out of there. Maybe it's better that they don't know.

Your Zlata

Dear Mimmy,

Nedo is back. You see, Mimmy, I was right and Daddy was wrong. Nedo was in Split with his girlfriend, who came from Austria. She came to Split just to see him. He says he felt slightly lost, but he did swim in the sea (the sea, what's that?), he hasn't forgotten how to swim, he sunbathed (he has a tan), walked along the waterfront, went to cafés and ate all sorts of things. But he didn't forget us. Any of us. He brought a little something for everyone. I got a pair of flip-flops, two pairs of stockings that his girlfriend bought specially for me, a bar of "Milka" chocolate, and a bag of terrific sweets.

So Nedo is back with us again and together we'll get through these hard times of war.

We finally resolved the mouse problem today. It stepped onto the glue, got stuck and that was the end. The end of a mouse. The end of Mommy's sufferings. He brought some excitement into the house.

Cici has taken to us and keeps coming. But the tomcat doesn't. He's vain, but she keeps calling him, meowing for him, she can't sleep at night, she wants to go out. Nedo and Auntie Boda are planning to give her an aspirin tonight—a real aspirin. To calm down her female nerves. That's what the cat doctor said to do.

Zlata

Dear Mimmy,

I'm MISERABLE. It's boredom and depression. First, there's no school because it's Bairam. Second, we've lost even the little electricity we had with the cable, so no music, no movies, no light. It's back to darkness again, more darkness. Daddy listens to depressing news. Third, we've had terrible shelling since Thursday. Phooey! Yesterday, it pounded away from four in the morning until ten at night. There were three to four shells a minute. We went back down into the cellar. This morning they reported that UNPROFOR had counted 1,100 and something shells, but Nedo says that's just 60% because that's all UNPROFOR manages to count. That means around two thousand shells. I tell you, three to four a minute. That's why I'm depressed. Do we have to go through all this again? I'm sorry. I'm being rude. It's because I'm nervous! Don't be mad at me, I'll get over it.

See you. CIAO!
Love,
Fipa!

Tuesday, June 1, 1993

Dear Mimmy,

CIAO! As you can see, today is June 1, Maja's birthday, Bairam (Kurban),[7] Tuesday, and the second June 1 of the war. Yesterday I was a disaster; today I'm supposedly better. We just had dinner. Let me tell you that breakfast, lunch and dinner were all uncooked because the gas went off yesterday. And as you know, we have no electricity either, so we're all on the verge of suicide. DISASTER! Oh, Mimmy, I can't take it anymore. I'm sick of everything. I'm so tired of all these Sssss! I'm sorry I'm swearing but I really can't take it anymore. It really is enough. There's a growing possibility of my killing myself, if all these morons up there and down here don't kill me first. I'm losing it. I WANT TO SCREAM, BANG MY FISTS, KILL! I'm human too, you know, I can only take so much. Ooohhh! I'm so sick of it all!

What's written here at the bottom was written

[7] Kurban-Bairam is the second of the Muslims' two Bairam religious holidays; rams *(kurbani)* are slaughtered for this second Bairam.

in a better mood.[x] I'm going to burst into tears!
Love,
Fipa

Dear Mimmy,

God, it's June already. I got an A on my math test today, so I'm HAPPY. But I have biology to study, so I'm UNHAPPY.

I've started going out with some of the girls in my class, Mimmy. But . . . it's not the real thing, I mean it's not what it was.

Cici calmed down after taking that aspirin, but the tomcat still hasn't come back. What a rude tomcat. First he seduces her and then he drops her. That's really not fair.
Zlata

Dear Mimmy,

It's exactly 9:30. Daddy is trying to get *Deutsche Welle*

---

[x] See page 135. Above the arrow pointing to a can of Pepsi, Zlata has written: "AAAAAH—IT'S POURING OUT!"

on the radio. Nejra is pounding away on the piano, singing a song she just thought up. Mommy is at work and I'm at home. As you can see, I'm not at school.

I got up at seven this morning—washed, brushed my teeth, got dressed, took my iron and vitamin pills and went to school. And what did I find? Only a handful of children. The only teachers there were Vlasta and the art teacher and they told us—NO SCHOOL. That's what they had been told. Was there going to be more shelling again? No classes here or at music school, so here I am at home. Bored. I don't know what to write to you.

Hey, Mimmy, I just thought of something. On Tuesday I saw something incredible. I saw Ismar Resic. He was in love with me in fourth grade but he "cooled off" in fifth. He sat in front of Mirna and me. He was small, Mimmy, smaller than me, and now he's 5'7" (100%). He's enormous. And you should hear his voice. Deeeep! And it's breaking, it must be puberty. You wouldn't believe it. All day Tuesday I kept saying: "Oh, if only you could see him," and "You know how big he is?"

UNBELIEVABLE!

Zlata

Sunday, June 13, 1993

Dear Mimmy,

Today I received five copies of YOU. They printed part of what I wrote to you, that's to say they photocopied my writing. My photograph is on the front cover, and there's an eye on the back. Not bad! But, I mustn't show off!

I have to tell you that yesterday was Mikica's birthday, and I wished her a happy birthday on the phone (the wartime way), because there was shelling again.

Cici hasn't been sleeping at home for the past few nights. She's taken off. Cici has given herself over to her love life. She's out with the boys.

Zlata

Tuesday, June 22, 1993

Dear Mimmy,

Today is the first or second day of summer, it depends which way you look at it. My life, Mimmy, is one of no electricity, no water, no gas, school which isn't school, rice, macaroni, a bit of green from Melica's garden, the occasional sweets, my piano, and, of course, you, Mimmy.

A puppy came to Alma and Dado's today. It's so

sweet. It's yellow, with white socks, a white patch on its chest, white nose. Cici is jealous because it ate up all her food.

I liked it and thought it would be nice to keep it, but that's impossible these days. We don't have enough food for ourselves.

Ciao!

Zlata

Saturday, June 26, 1993

Dear Mimmy,

Two pieces of sad news. First, Alma and Dado returned the puppy. It's a small pincher and Alma wants a big dog she can walk around the neighborhood.

OOOOOH!

The other sad news is that Nedo is leaving. He's going on vacation and he said he won't be coming back, he's going to run away. The "creep." We've all grown so fond of him and now he's leaving. But, it's better that way. Now we'll "have somebody to send us packages and everything." Still, I'm really sorry he's going. We've all come to love him, and he us, and now we're parting. There he is, he's calling me, I have to go. NEVER MIND, KEEP GOING,

ZLATA, AND TRY NOT TO BE A CRYBABY!
CIAO, Mimmy,
Love,
Zlata

Dear Mimmy,
Two pieces of news. One incredible, one "so-so."

First the "so-so" one. Yesterday, when I was going down the stairs to the Bobars' I sprained my leg. My leg simply went that-a-way and snapped. I didn't go to school today because I can't stand on my foot, so I'm lying down. I can't stand and I can't walk. Compresses. Lasonil cream, I suppose I'll survive. Now the second (incredible) piece of news. The book promotion was supposed to be yesterday. But the gas went off—the generators aren't working (you see, gas remembers), and the invitations can't be printed. So I tell everybody: "NO PROMOTION."

I've been thinking about Nedo leaving. I keep telling myself "Oh, he won't go," but then I sober up and I feel bad, so bad. Is he really going to leave?

Slobo has gone to Subotica for further medical treatment. I guess he'll finally be reunited with Doda and Dejan?
Your Zlata

Dear Mimmy,

What I wrote you about Nedo leaving, well it's happened. He left last night. He was working a lot these past few days, I hardly saw him.

He came at around eight o'clock last night to have our picture taken together and say goodbye. And all that, in half an hour. At eight-thirty he simply said: "OK, time for a kiss," and smack, smack, smack, "don't cry, take care of yourselves, you take care of yourself too, write and send me some photos." BANG! The door slammed shut and it was all over. Nedo was gone!

Everything has a beginning and an end, and so had this wonderful time I've spent with Nedo.

After that BANG I went BOO-HOO! SNIFFLE! SNIFFLE!. And everyone kept saying to me: "Don't cry, Fipa, he's going to a better place, imagine what it's like for him . . . ," where, oh, where is my hanky? I know, I know, but I'm still sorry. BOO-HOO! SNIFFLE!

I calmed down and began thinking. Thinking brought back memories: "Hey, you remember when . . . ," "He really was a wonderful guy . . . ," "Nedo is . . . ," and so on and so forth.

I find it hard, I'm really sad, but I think it must be hardest for Auntie Boda. First Maja and Bojana, and now her adopted son, Nedo. I don't know, everything is so stupid, let's go kill ourselves! Let's, Mimmy.

Love,

Zlata

Dear Mimmy,

Well, now I'm left without Nedo as well. Slowly everybody is leaving while I stay behind. God, Mimmy, will I ever get out of this hell-hole? I've had more than enough. Nedo's departure reminded me that all my friends have left.

I'm sitting in my room. Cici is with me. She's enjoying herself on the armchair—sleeping. As for me, I'm reading through my letters. Letters are all I've got left of my friends. I read them and they take me back to my friends.

> I have to tell you that I miss you, but I hope we'll see each other soon. I'm slowly getting used to this new life. Take care of yourself, Zlata, and be good to your parents.
> Much love from your Matea

> Dear Fipa, I think of you often and wonder what you're doing, how you're living. I miss you a lot,

I miss the whole of Sarajevo—the most beautiful city in the world, with the biggest and warmest embrace in the world, the heart of the world. It's now in flames, but it will never burn down. I know it's hard for you. All I can say is that I love and miss you.

Many, many kisses from your Martina and all the other refugees who want to come home!

I heard two of Dr. Alban's songs: "It's My Life" and "Say Hallelujah." I don't know if they've managed to come your way. Maja thought today of taping a cassette for you with hit songs by Mick Jagger, Michael Jackson, Bon Jovi. Nothing new in the fashion world. Oh, Fipa, how I wish I could talk to you.

Much love from your Bojana

I'm sending these "Pretty Ladies" to my Fipa so she can see what people will be wearing this summer and what they'll be dishing out all their money for. Naturally, each of these "pretty ladies" carries a million kisses for my Fipa and will tell her how much Maja loves and thinks of her.

My Dear Zlata,
You are and always will be my best friend. No one

will ever be able to destroy our friendship, not even this war. Although you're in Sarajevo and I'm in Italy, although we haven't seen each other for more than a year now, you are still my best friend.

Much love from your Oga

My Darling Little Girl,
I'm sending you this flower from our garden and this butterfly from the woods. You can make a picture with them. If I could, I'd send you a basket full of flowers, the forest, trees and lots of birds, but these people here won't let me. So I'm sending you my love with the gentle butterfly and the red flower.

Don't worry about the future. Remember that good and happy times come to all good people, and you and your parents are good people and you will be well, cheerful and happy. I think of you often.

Much love from your Keka

And so, Mimmy, in their letters they send me their love, their thoughts, pictures of a normal life, songs, fashion, best wishes for happiness and an end to this madness. I read them and sometimes I cry, because I want *them,* I want life, not just letters.

Now all I'll have left of Nedo, too, are letters. Still, letters mean a lot to me, I look forward to them.
Ciao!
Zlata

Tuesday, July 13, 1993

Dear Mimmy,
I'm sick again. I have a temperature, a tummy ache and a sore throat. The thermometer and medicine are by my side. God, why do I have to be sick on top of everything else? I miss Nedo and am waiting for your book promotion.
Your Zlata

Thursday, July 15, 1993

Dear Mimmy,
Today I heard that the promotion is on Saturday. Yes, Saturday. And here I am sick. What will it be like, Mimmy?

Saturday, July 17, 1993

Dear Mimmy,
PROMOTION DAY,
Since I didn't take you with me (just a part of you was there) I have to tell you what it was like.

It was wonderful. The presenter was a girl who looked unbelievably like Linda Evangelista. She read parts of you, Mimmy, and was even accompanied on the piano. Auntie Irena was there. Warm and kind, as always, with warm words for children and adults alike.

It was held in the café Jež, and was packed with wonderful people, family, friends, school friends and, of course, NEIGHBORS. There was electricity (a generator), and the lightbulbs made it all even nicer. You and I, Mimmy, have Gordana Trebinjac of the International Peace Center to thank for the good organization, and for having made it as nice as it was.

Naturally, there were film cameras and photographers and a huge bouquet of flowers, roses and daisies, for us, Mimmy.

At the end I read my message. This is what I said:

Suddenly, unexpectedly, someone is using the ugly powers of war, which horrify me, to try to pull and drag me away from the shores of peace, from the happiness of wonderful friendships, playing and love. I feel like a swimmer who was made to enter the cold water, against her will. I feel shocked, sad, unhappy and frightened and I wonder where they are forcing me to go, I wonder why they have taken away my peaceful and lovely shores of my childhood. I used to rejoice at each new day, because each was beautiful in its own way. I used to rejoice at the sun, at playing, at songs. In short, I enjoyed my childhood. I had no need of a better one. I have less and less strength to keep swimming in these cold waters. So take me back to the shores of my childhood, where I was warm, happy and content, like all the children whose childhood and the right to enjoy it are now being destroyed.

The only thing I want to say to everyone is: PEACE!

There was a Spaniard at the promotion—Julio Fuentos. He photographed me standing on some jerrycans (full of water—a precious liquid in Sarajevo), and the woman to whom they belonged almost went crazy. "OOOHHHH, just so long as the jerrycans don't break!" They didn't!

All in all, it was nice. It couldn't have been otherwise, since it was your promotion, Mimmy. I represented you. You know how much I love you. I represented you with all the love I feel for you.

When I got home that afternoon, Auntie Radmila brought me a big flowerpot wrapped in colorful paper and tied up with a bow. Inside the pot was a tomato, a real live tomato. That was the nicest "bouquet" I ever got.

Love,
Zlata

Friday, July 23, 1993

Dear Mimmy,

Even since July 17, various people have been coming around—journalists, reporters, cameramen. From Spain, France, the US, England . . . and yesterday a crew came from ABC News. They filmed me for American TV as the "person of the week." Hey, imagine, me a personality?

They filmed me in my room, by my piano, in my apartment with my parents. They talked to me. In English, of course. I have to boast and tell you that they told me my English is EXCELLENT.

And tonight the world will be looking at me (and that, you know, is because of you, Mimmy). Meanwhile I'm looking at the candle, and all around me is darkness. I'm looking in the dark.

Can that outside world see the darkness I see? Just as I can't see myself on TV tonight, so the rest of the world probably can't see the darkness I'm looking at. We're at two ends of the world. Our lives are so different. Theirs is a bright light. Ours is darkness.

Your Zlata

P.S. You know that Cici is pregnant? She's going to have kittens. I have to "get" Mommy and Daddy to take one.

Zlata

Tuesday, July 27, 1993

Dear Mimmy,

Journalists, reporters, TV and radio crews from all over the world (even Japan). They're interested in you, Mimmy, and ask me about you, but also about me. It's exciting. Nice. Unusual for a wartime child.

My days have changed a little. They're more interesting now. It takes my mind off things. When I go to bed at night I think about the day behind me. Nice, as though it weren't wartime, and with such thoughts I happily fall asleep.

But in the morning, when the wheels of the water carts wake me up, I realize that there's a war on, that mine is a wartime life. SHOOTING, NO ELECTRICITY, NO WATER, NO GAS, NO FOOD. Almost no life.

Zlata

Dnevnik rada

Dear Mimmy,

iako je sam napisala da ne vjerujem da će se 21.09.'93. god. desiti nešto lijepo, ipak je u meni treperila želja da se to dogodi. Ali - badava.

Politika mi i dalje zagrčava ŽIVOT 8!

Dear
Mimmy,

voli te tvoja

Zlata

SUBOTA, 25.9.'93.

Dear Mimmy,

struja je došla, ali se dijeli po planu redukcije. A redukcija, kao i cijeli ovaj ži-

WILD AT HEART

24 08 90

"I will try to get through all this, with your support, Mimmy, hoping that it will all pass and...that I will be a child again, living my childhood in peace."

Friday, July 30, 1993

Dear Mimmy,

A journalist has just left. I'm at the window. It's hot.
I am watching the people lug water home.

You should see the different kinds of water carts
they have. How inventive people are. Two-wheelers,
three-wheelers, wheelbarrows, shopping carts,
wheelchairs, hospital tables, supermarket carts and,
topping them all—a sled on rollerskates. And you
should hear the sounds! The various sounds and
screeching of the wheels. That is what wakes us up
every morning. It's all funny and sad at the same
time. Sometimes I think about all the films that
could be made in Sarajevo. There are loads of subjects for films here.

Love,

Zlata

Monday, August 2, 1993

Dear Mimmy,

More journalists, reporters and cameramen. They
write, take photographs, film, and it all goes to
France, Italy, Canada, Japan, Spain, America. But
you and I, Mimmy, we stay where we are, we stay and
we wait, and, of course, keep each other company.

Some people compare me with Anne Frank. That

frightens me, Mimmy. I don't want to suffer her fate.

Zlata

Dear Mimmy,

All these journalists got me muddled and I forgot to tell you that school is over (July 4, 1993). Sixth year is behind me. It was a wartime school year.

Mirna slept over last night. There was no shooting, but there's no electricity or water. THERE IS GAS! YESSS!

The gas came on at about 4:00 today. It's now 7:40 and we still have gas. As for electricity, we haven't had any for a LONG, LONG TIME. There has been no electricity, no water and no bread for three months.

Just try and imagine what it's like, Mimmy. Every day is hard.

We make do with candles and oil lamps instead of electricity, we lug water, the wood stove (what wood?) replaces the oven. AND BREAD. Bread is the biggest problem. You can only get flour for foreign money. And in order to bake it, we have to find a free oven in the neighborhood.

Rushing, running, worrying—all day long.

Imagine, Mimmy, it's August, and we're heating.
Zlata

Sunday, August 8, 1993

Dear Mimmy,

We got a letter from Keka, and Martina and Matea today. We were so excited. We laughed but, yes, there were also tears. They're fine. Martina and Matea are growing, living, eating . . . Ah, while on the subject of food, today I made Mommy, Daddy and Mirna laugh when I said I'd like to eat something oily, salty, sugary, in other words something "unhealthy" so that when my tummy hurts at least I know why. Something like a sandwich (but a real sandwich). YUM-YUM!

Mirna is sleeping over again tonight. I told her that I've had enough already (ha, ha, ha) and that she's really a pain (tee-hee-hee). She has to practice because tomorrow we have two piano lessons and solfeggio as well. Exams are coming up.

Tuesday, August 10, 1993

Dear Mimmy,

I have more very, very sad news for you. OUR CAT

IS NO MORE. Our Cici died. Awful. First Cicko, and now Cici.

I went to Auntie Boda's today and talked about all sorts of things. How I got a C in solfeggio, how I got a pair of trousers from Auntie Irena, how my piano exam was coming up. And I asked why they hadn't come over the night before.

Auntie Boda: "We had a problem."

Me (stupidly): "Whyyy?"

Auntie Boda: "We don't have our cat anymore."

Me (lost): "You, you mean it's d-d-dead???"

Me (a lump in my throat): "I have to go. I'm going home, I have to go home. Goodbye."

And when I got home: BOO-HOO! SOB! SOB! SOB! OOOHHH!

Mommy and Daddy (in duet): "What's wrong??"

Me: "The cat, the cat. It died."

Mommy and Daddy (again in duet): "Aaaaaah!!!"

And then an hour of tears. Can it be? Our cat, the most wonderful, most beautiful, most lovable, sweetest, best cat in the whole wide world—gone. My little cat. When I think of how lovable, sweet and wonderful she was! I cry my eyes out. I know terrible things are happening, people are being killed, there's a war on, but still . . . I'm so sorry. She cheered us all up, made us smile, filled up our hours. Yellow Cici. My friend.

Haris and Enes buried her in the yard next to Cicko. They made a little grave out of tiles. She deserved it.

I'm very, very sad.

Zlata

Wednesday, August 11, 1993

Dear Mimmy,

Today is the first day without Cici. I miss her so much. We're all sad. We talk about her, remember how lovable and beautiful she was.

She died because she was pregnant and couldn't produce her litter. Oh, Cici, it's all that tomcat's fault. And I was looking forward to getting a kitten.

Your Zlata

Friday, August 13, 1993

Dear Mimmy,

The days go by without Cici. You have to keep living.

Today I got my report card. I finished the sixth grade with straight As.

On Monday I probably have my piano exam.
I'm nervous about it.
Zlata

Sunday, August 15, 1993

Dear Mimmy,
We received a letter from Maja, Bojana and Nedo.
Nedo is now in Austria—in Vienna. They're together there now. It's a short letter, their thoughts
are with us just as ours are with them.

And now the news. Nedo is getting married on
August 26. Maja is going to be the bridesmaid. Oh,
I wish I could be there!
Your Zlata

Tuesday, August 17, 1993

Dear Mimmy,
Journalists, television reporters, cameramen keep
coming. I've already come to know quite a few of
them. Some come back. There's Alexandra, Paul,
Ron, Kevin . . . I've become fond of them. Alexandra took my picture today standing next to the
UNPROFOR building. I was with Mirna.

I forgot to tell you that we're in the grips of

"gasomania." We're getting a gas pipe installed. But will there be any gas???

Electricity is returning to the city. But our crooks, our criminals, our thieves stole the oil from the transformer station, and now almost no one has electricity. Can you imagine? They use the oil in place of gas to drive their cars.

Your Zlata

Wednesday, August 18, 1993

Dear Mimmy,

Yesterday I heard some optimistic news. The "kids" have signed an agreement in Geneva on the demilitarization of Sarajevo. What can I say? That I hope, that I believe it???? I don't know how I could. Whenever I believed and hoped for something it didn't happen, and whenever I didn't believe or expect anything it did happen.

Today some Italian journalists asked me what I thought about the idea of "Sarajevo—an Open City." I gave them some answer, but I think the "kids" are just playing and I don't believe them at all and I've had enough of everything. Because, I know there is no electricity, no water, no food, that people keep getting killed, that we no longer have even candles, that smuggling and crime are rife, that the days are getting shorter and soon it will be what the whole of Sarajevo fears most: WINTER. The mere thought of it gives me the chills.

Mommy and Daddy often say: *"Post nubila, Phoebus,"* which is Latin, Mimmy, and it means: "After the clouds comes the sun." But when????
Zlata

Thursday, August 19, 1993

Dear Mimmy,
Mirna had her piano exam today. She got an A. It looks as though I'll have mine tomorrow. I have to practice.

There's no gas again. But there is talk that the electricity might return tomorrow. We'll see.
Zlata

Saturday, August 21, 1993

Dear Mimmy,
Everybody is in a bad mood these days. Mommy, Daddy, Braco, Melica, Grandma, Granddad . . . I don't know, everybody's quite edgy.

Did I tell you, Mimmy, that Kenan (Melica's son) is in the hospital? Wait, wait, no, he's not wounded. There's no injury. He's sick. He has jaundice. From the water, probably, because they get their water from a spring and it looks as if that spring isn't "pure." And there seems to be an epidemic in that part of town.

Mirna was here yesterday. Even she isn't quite right.

The day before yesterday I was at my cousin Diana's. We watched two movies: *Purple Rain* and *Breakfast at Tiffany's*. Audrey Hepburn is really cute. Do you know she died? Yes, she died about two months ago, maybe more.

Yesterday I got an A in my piano exam. Super.

The political situation? A STUPID MESS. Maybe that's why everybody is so edgy. The "kids" are trying to come to some agreement again. They're drawing maps, coloring with their crayons, but I think they're crossing out human beings, childhood and everything that's nice and normal. They really are just like kids.

There's no mail. I don't know why, but nobody has been getting any mail lately.
Zlata

Thursday, August 26, 1993

Dear Mimmy,
Our Nedo is getting married today. Yes, our Nedo.

Today is what Bojana calls "Judgment Day." Today he stops being a bachelor and becomes a "family man." Ha, ha, ha!

We had a little celebration here in honor of Nedo's wedding. Mommy made a cake (hey, a cake?) in the shape of a heart. Sweet. Auntie Boda and Alemka made the rest, whatever you can make in these wartime conditions—sandwiches, little rolls, a savory pie (a little rice, a little mangel and you've got yourself a good pie) . . .

We all got together at Auntie Boda's. Nedo was in Vienna. But we were with him in our thoughts and wished him and Amna every happiness. An imitation wedding, Mimmy, that's what it was—an imitation of life. People in Sarajevo do it all the time. We imitate life to make things easier.

I find it so strange, so odd that Nedo is getting married. Auntie Boda sent a card with the names of all his neighbors and friends from Sarajevo, and at the end she wrote:—"Just our little yellow pussy-cat is missing. She has passed away." Yes, but we're learning to steel ourselves, this war is teaching us, and we're slowly suppressing everything that hurts us.

Your Zlata

Dear Mimmy,

Yesterday Nedo got married, and yesterday Auntie Radmila and Uncle Tomo left Sarajevo. They left Sarajevo forever. They had lost their apartment and everything in it. They were living in somebody else's apartment, then they got lodgers. They've been separated from their children from the start of the war. They have gone to join their daughters and start a new life somewhere. I'm sorry Auntie Radmila has gone. She was wonderful to me. She'd often surprise me with a sweet, chewing gum, powdered milk, fruit, a warm word and, of course, there was that wonderful "bouquet," the tomato in the flowerpot.

Mommy is very sad. Now Auntie Radmila has also gone. Mommy has only Auntie Ivanka left now. But I think that she and Uncle Mirko will be leaving soon too. And so, Mimmy, our friends are leaving. We say goodbye to them and we stay behind.
Ciao!
Zlata

Thursday, September 2, 1993

Dear Mimmy,
Alexandra (the reporter from *Le Figaro*) came. She

came to say goodbye and to take a few more photos. I've grown very fond of her and in these few meetings we've become real friends.

She was in Mostar and she's very sad. She says Mostar looks terrible. In fact, it doesn't exist anymore. Such a beautiful town and it doesn't exist anymore. She was very upset by what she saw in Mostar.

The talk in town is that Sarajevo will suffer the same fate. I'm afraid, Mimmy. You see, other things are now important. Now force rules and it can do anything. It can wipe out people, families, towns. I keep asking myself for the hundred millionth time: WHY? WHY ME? WHY? WHY IS THIS HAPPENING???

Alexandra is going home, she's going back to her peaceful country, her peaceful town, to her friends and her job. She has so much. AND ME? I have a burned-down, destroyed country, a demolished town, friends-refugees all over the world ... But, luckily, I have you Mimmy, and your lined pages, which are always silent, patiently waiting for me to fill them out with my sad thoughts.

I went with Alexandra to the old Sarajevo library, the Vječnica. Generations and generations of people enriched their knowledge by reading and leafing through its countless books. Somebody once said that books are the greatest treasure, the greatest friend one has. The Vječnica was such a treasure trove. We had so many friends there. But now we've lost the treasure and the friends and the lovely old building. They all went up in the destroying flames.

The Vječnica is now a treasure trove of ashes, bricks, and the odd scrap of paper. I brought home a piece of brick and a fragment of metal as a memento of that treasure-house of friends.

I said goodbye to Alexandra and said I hoped to see her again.

Your Zlata

Saturday, September 4, 1993

Dear Mimmy,

Yesterday was a bit iffy. A man was wounded on the bridge by a sniper. Perviz's gas-pressure regulator got stolen. The apartment now has gas (pipes, not the gas itself). I'm worried about the electricity. Food—? When the real winter starts we'll turn on the storage heater. Absolutely no mail is coming in, not even through UNPROFOR. Aaaaah. Samra got married yesterday. The lucky man is Zijo (his only fault: a limp handshake)! Mommy and I went to attend the "solemn act of marriage between Samra Kozarić and Zijad Pehid," as the registrar would say.

The registrar rushed everything so much that I couldn't get what was happening. Afterward everybody went to lunch at the Premier, and Mommy and I went home to our MISHMASH, but it was a good "mishmash," a good one.

Well, Mimmy, that's it!

Lots of love,

Zlata

Sunday, September 5, 1993

Dear Mimmy,

All eyes and ears are turned on Geneva. More agreements, negotiations. I don't think this will ever end. My childhood, youth and life are slipping away while I wait. We stand as witnesses who didn't deserve to have to live through all this.

Today we heard that letters aren't coming into Sarajevo anymore. There's something worse than not having electricity, water and gas, and that's not getting letters, which are our only contact with the outside world. Now we've lost that as well. It's just too much!

Žika brought me something wonderful today. A real live orange. Mommy said: "Let's see whether I remember how to peel it?" And, and . . . she remembered. She did it. It was so nice and juicy. YUMMY!

The other day we went to Djoka's (Bojana and Merica's father). I went to see whether any of their shoes would fit me, because all of mine are too small. I didn't find any. Everything is standing still, it's just me that's growing, Mimmy.

We heard some sad news from Djoko. Slobo's condition is deteriorating and he's been moved to the Military Hospital in Belgrade. Doda and Dejan have left for Slovenia. They've split up on various sides again. The sad fate of a family.

Ciao!

Zlata

Monday, September 6, 1993

Dear Mimmy,

The first day of the new school year. I'm starting seventh grade. New subjects, new knowledge, new obligations, new school days, but I don't feel the way I used to. It's probably the war again.

Pupils from four years are all in one classroom. Some listen to their language lessons, others to biology, others to English and still others to chemistry. It's awful, Mimmy. It makes me sad. Don't I deserve

to go to a normal school? What have I done not to deserve it?
Your Zlata

Wednesday, September 8, 1993
Dear Mimmy,
Today, today I received a letter. A letter from my friend in Vienna. A letter from my Nedo. It made me so happy! I don't have to tell you, you know what it's like.

> My darling Fipa,
> I'm so sorry I wasn't at the promotion of your Diary, but I have my own copy and won't give it to anyone to read (maybe I will, but only in my presence).
>
> I have to admit it was very, very hard for me too, when I had to leave. I acted "cool," but I had a lump in my throat and couldn't even talk. Half of me is still there with you. But one day we'll meet again and laugh at all the things that bothered us, a little or a lot.
>
> Keep your feet on the ground and your head out of the clouds.
> Much love to you from your Nedo

There, that's part of Nedo's letter, which I keep on my desk. I keep rereading it. I'm going to learn it by heart like all the others. And so Nedo's letter will join my "war archive."

Paul (the journalist) came to say goodbye today. He's leaving for London. I was at school and so I couldn't say goodbye to him. But he said he'd be back at the end of September. We'll see each other again. I'm glad, because Paul has become another dear friend. Ciao Paul, until we meet again!

Zlata

Thursday, September 9, 1993

Dear Mimmy,

Today is Mommy's birthday. I gave her a biiiig kiss and a "Happy Birthday, Mommy." That's all I have.

This is Mommy's second birthday in wartime. My birthday is coming up too. December is near. Will it be another wartime birthday? Again????

Your Zlata

Wednesday, September 15, 1993

Dear Mimmy,

Back to the old story. There was gunfire yesterday and we all immediately got nervous. We remembered the cellar and were afraid of going through it all over again. I sincerely hope we won't have to. But hoping doesn't mean a thing here.

I'm going to UNPROFOR at the Skenderija building tomorrow—to the dentist's. All the children in the neighborhood have been, and now it's my turn.

School! I'm disappointed. There are lots of children who missed a school year last year. I don't feel like a real seventh-grader either. I feel as if I'm still in fifth grade, the way I was that April, not so long ago in 1992. Time seems to have stopped since then.

The books aren't mine and they're not new. Some are Bojana's, some Martina's, some Diana's, and some Mirna gave me. The pencils are old, the notebooks half full, from last year. The war has ruined even school and school life.

I'm now in the sixth year of music school. The teacher told me to practice every day, and knuckle down. It's the final year. It has to be taken seriously.

Lots of journalists, reporters and TV crews from France are coming tomorrow. Maybe Alexandra and Christian will come. I already miss them.
Your Zlata

Dear Mimmy,

The "kids" are negotiating something, signing something. Again giving us hope that this madness will end. There's supposed to be a cease-fire tomorrow and on September 21 at Sarajevo airport everybody is supposed to sign FOR PEACE. Will the war stop on the day that marks the change from one season to another???

With all the disappointments I've had with previous truces and signatures, I can't believe it.

I can't believe it because another horrible shell fell today, ending the life of a three-year-old little boy, wounding his sister and mother.

All I know is that the result of their little games is 15,000 dead in Sarajevo, 3,000 of them children, 50,000 permanent invalids, whom I already see in the streets on crutches, in wheelchairs, armless and legless. And I know that there's no room left in the cemeteries and parks to bury the latest victims.

Maybe that's why this madness should stop.

Your Zlata

Dear Mimmy,

I keep thinking about Sarajevo, and the more I think about it, the more it seems to me that Sarajevo is slowly ceasing to be what it was. So many dead and wounded. Historical monuments destroyed. Treasure troves of books and paintings gone. Century-old trees felled. So many people have left Sarajevo forever. No birds, just the occasional chirping sparrow. A dead city. And the warlords are still negotiating over something, drawing, crossing out, I just don't know for how long. Until September 29? I don't believe it!

Your Zlata

Monday, September 20, 1993

Dear Mimmy,

All eyes and ears are on tomorrow's game of War or Peace. Everybody is waiting for that historic meeting at Sarajevo airport. Suddenly, unexpected news. The Serbian, Croatian and Muslim warlords have met on a warship in the Adriatic. For another shipwreck? We'll find out!

Your Zlata

Tuesday, September 21, 1993

Dear Mimmy,

The historic game of WAR OR PEACE has been postponed. Does that mean PEACE is losing again? I'm really fed up with politics!

Your Zlata

Wednesday, September 22, 1993

Dear Mimmy,

Although I told you that I didn't think anything good would happen on September 21, 1993, I still had a flicker of hope that it would. But it was no use.

Another D-Day has come and gone. How many have we had? A hundred? A million? How many more will there be?

Politics is making my life miserable!!

Your Zlata

Saturday, September 25, 1993

Dear Mimmy,

The electricity is back, but it's being rationed. And the rationing, like the life we're living, is stupid. We get four hours of electricity every fifty-six hours.

You should see, Mimmy, what a madhouse this is when the electricity comes on! Piles of unwashed laundry waiting to go into the washing machine. Even bigger piles of laundry waiting for the iron. Dust waiting to be vacuumed. Cooking to be done, bread to be baked, and we'd all like to watch a bit of television. There's hair to be washed and dried with a hair dryer. It's incredible. You wouldn't believe it.

Every time Mommy says: "If we're not going to have electricity, then let's not have any at all. That way I don't worry. This is unbearable." Yes, but then again, Mommy . . .

We have water more often now.

There's a problem with bread again, even though the electricity is back. We get 300 grams per person every three days. Ridiculous!

I had to laugh at lunch today when Daddy said: "This 'German' lunch is good." You must be wondering, Mimmy, why we would be eating a "German lunch." The potato salad was made of potatoes and onions bought for Deutsche Marks at our "rich" market. With it we had German fish from the humanitarian aid package. So that's "German," isn't it?

Your Zlata

We waited for September 27 and 28. The 27th was the Assembly of Bosnian Intellectuals, and the 28th was the session of the B-H Parliament. And the result is "conditional acceptance of the Geneva agreement." CONDITIONAL. What does that mean? To me, it means non-acceptance of the agreement, because there's no peace. To me it means the continuation of the war and everything that goes with it.

Once more the circle closes. The circle is closing, Mimmy, and it's strangling us.

Sometimes I wish I had wings so I could fly away from this hell.

Like Icarus.

There's no other way.

But to do that I'd need wings for Mommy, wings for Daddy, for Grandma and Granddad and . . . for you, Mimmy.

And that's impossible, because humans are not birds.

That's why I have to try to get through all this, with your support, Mimmy, and to hope that it will pass and that I will not suffer the fate of Anne Frank. That I will be a child again, living my childhood in peace.
Love,
Zlata

Dear Mimmy,

Life in a closed circle continues. You wonder what that life is like, Mimmy. It's a life of waiting, of fear, a life where you want the circle to open and the sun of peace to shine down on you again.

Today, while I was playing the piano, Mommy came into the room and told me I had visitors. I went into the sitting room and there I found ALEX-ANDRA. She came from Paris this morning. Rested, beautiful, content. I was glad to see her. And I must say I missed her, because she really is wonderful. She's here in Sarajevo again now, so we'll spend some time together.

Zlata

Thursday, October 7, 1993

Dear Mimmy,

Things are the way they used to be, lately. There's no shooting (thank God), I go to school, read, play the piano . . .

Winter is approaching, but we have nothing to heat with.

I look at the calendar and it seems as though this year of 1993 will again be marked by war. God, we've lost two years listening to gunfire, battling with electricity, water, food, and waiting for peace.

I look at Mommy and Daddy. In two years they've aged ten. And me? I haven't aged, but I've grown, although I honestly don't know how. I don't eat fruit or vegetables, I don't drink juices, I don't eat meat . . . I am a child of rice, peas and spaghetti. There I am talking about food again. I often catch myself dreaming about chicken, a good cutlet, pizza, lasagna . . . Oh, enough of that.

Zlata

Tuesday, October 12, 1993

Dear Mimmy,

I don't remember whether I told you that last summer I sent a letter through school to a pen-pal in America. It was a letter for an American girl or boy.

Today I got an answer. A boy wrote to me. His name is Brandon, he's twelve like me, and lives in Harrisburg, Pennsylvania. It really made me happy.

I don't know who invented the mail and letters, but thank you whoever you are. I now have a friend in America, and Brandon has a friend in Sarajevo. This is my first letter from across the Atlantic. And in it is a reply envelope, and a lovely pencil.

A Canadian TV crew and journalist from *The Sunday Times* (Janine) came to our gym class today. They brought me two chocolate bars. What a treat. It's been a long time since I've had sweets.

Love,

Zlata

Wednesday, October 13, 1993

Dear Mimmy,

Today we received a letter from Oga and Jaca in Italy. They sent us photos. Oga has grown into a young girl, and you can see from the letter that she's more serious and mature now. I could barely recognize her. When Mommy saw the picture she began to cry. The letter really made us happy. It was sent in August, and took a long, long time to reach us.

They also read you, Mimmy (I sent them a copy in a letter), and say that they cried and laughed as they read.

Here's what Oga writes:

I often think of us on Mount Jahorina. But that's just a lovely memory now. Skiing, sledding down the road, making snow houses, gossiping before going to sleep, birthday parties, New Year's Eve.

Those are all lovely memories of the good times we had, which were suddenly cut short, never to be repeated.

All the houses on Jahorina have been looted, everything down to the counters has been removed. Imagine the idiots. They could have at least moved some refugees into those houses.

I'd find it hard to look at. We're left with only our memories.

I tried to imagine those abandoned houses overgrown with grass. And I have to tell you, Mimmy, that I got a lump in my throat. War has destroyed Jahorina as well, and all the lovely times we spent there.

They've invited me to come and be with them in Italy, because I don't deserve to be here. I'd love to go, but it's impossible. Nobody can leave this cursed town.

The shooting has died down, there's hardly any gunfire at all right now, and Mommy and Daddy keep thinking about the future. They say there is none in this town. That's what many people think. But it's impossible to leave this town.

Love,

Zlata

Dear Mimmy,

Those lunatics up in the hills must have read what I wrote about the shooting yesterday. They want to show me that they're still around. They went SHOOTING today. Shells fell around the marketplace, and we don't know how Grandma and Granddad are. Poor things. These lunatics haven't just stolen from us our childhood, they've stolen from my grandparents and other old people a peaceful old age. They're not letting them live out the rest of their lives in peace. They had to ruin that too.

I didn't have classes or music school today. They sent us home, so I'll spend the whole day at home reading, playing the piano, spending some time with Nejra and Haris. I was supposed to go to Mirna's today, but they spoiled that for me.

I didn't tell you, Mimmy, that you're about to go out into the world. You're going to be published abroad. I allowed it, so you could tell the world what I wrote to you. I wrote to you about the war, about myself and Sarajevo in the war, and the world wants to know about it. I wrote what I felt, saw and heard, and now people outside of Sarajevo are going to know it. Have a good journey into the world.
Your Zlata

Dear Mimmy,

Yesterday our friends in the hills reminded us of their presence and that they are now in control and can kill, wound, destroy . . . yesterday was a truly horrible day.

Five hundred and ninety shells. From 4:30 in the morning on, throughout the day. Six dead and fifty six wounded. That is yesterday's toll. Souk-bunar fared the worst. I don't know how Melica is. They say that half the houses up there are gone.

We went down into the cellar. Into the cold, dark, stupid cellar which I hate. We were there for hours and hours. They kept pounding away. All the neighbors were with us.

AGAIN! Again and again they keep sinking all our boats, taking and burning all our hopes. People said that they wouldn't do it anymore. That there would soon be an end to it, that everything would resolve itself. THAT THIS STUPID WAR WOULD END!

Oh God, why do they spoil everything? Sometimes I think it would be better if they kept shooting, so that we wouldn't find it so hard when it starts up again. This way, just as you relax, it starts up AGAIN. I am convinced now that it will never end.

Because some people don't want it to, some evil people who hate children and ordinary folk.

I keep thinking that we're alone in this hell, that nobody is thinking of us, nobody is offering us a helping hand. But there are people who are thinking and worrying about us.

Yesterday the Canadian TV crew and Janine came to see how we had survived the mad shelling. That was nice of them. Really kind.

And when we saw that Janine was holding an armful of food, we got so sad we cried. Alexandra came too.

People worry about us, they think about us, but sub-humans want to destroy us. Why? I keep asking myself why?

We haven't done anything. We're innocent. But helpless!

Zlata

PJESME

boja teških godina.

Dva, tri metra snijega i tutanj ljigura,
pusti Ficu kad ne pali dok ga raja ne gura
Na ormaru dunje zrije
ja još čuvam za tebe

A na moru tamo, mljeko, varenika,
svima ravno do mora, a more Zelenika
Od Makarske do Neuma
uspomena ostala.

REF:

Ako pitaš...

... Nikome se ne pomori la!

Prepisivala:

Zlata Filipović